Physicians and Professional Behavior Management Strategies

A Leadership Roadmap and Guide with Case Studies

❖

By Matthew J. Mazurek, MD, MHA, CPE, FACHE, FASA

American Association for
PHYSICIAN
LEADERSHIP

Copyright © 2022 by Matthew J. Mazurek, MD, MHA, CPE, FACHE, FASA

Print 978-0-9966632-9-8

Ebook 979-8-9856044-0-5

Published by **American Association for Physician Leadership, Inc.**

PO Box 96503 | BMB 97493 | Washington, DC 20090-6503

Website: www.physicianleaders.org

AAPL books are available at special quantity discounts to use as premiums and sales promotions, or for use in corporate training programs. For more information, please write to Special Sales at journal@physicianleaders.org

This publication is designed to provide general information and is sold with the understanding that neither the author nor the publisher is engaged in rendering legal, accounting, ethical, or clinical advice. If legal or other expert advice is required, the services of a competent professional person should be sought.

13   8 7 6 5 4 3 2 1

Copyedited, typeset, indexed, and printed in the United States of America

PUBLISHER
Nancy Collins

EDITORIAL ASSISTANT
Jennifer Weiss

DESIGN & LAYOUT
Carter Publishing Studio

COPYEDITOR
Pat George

In loving memory of Dianne Ruehle, a teacher and friend who helped me grow as a human being.

TABLE OF CONTENTS

ABOUT THE AUTHOR

Dr. Matt Mazurek grew up in Fresno, California, and attended California State University, Fresno. After two years as a physics major, he switched to English literature and studied poetry writing with Pulitzer Prize-winning poet Philip Levine, Peter Everwine, and Charles Hanzlicek. After earning his BA *magna cum laude,* he edited the poetry section of *The San Joaquin Review.* Prior to matriculating to medical school at the University of California, San Francisco, he taught astronomy at Fresno State and physics at a local high school in Fresno.

As a medical student, Mazurek won a grant through Genentech to study the mechanisms of action of volatile anesthetics in C. Spencer Yost's lab at UCSF. Mazurek's work culminated in his being named a finalist for the Dean's Prize in student research. He co-authored two papers, one on the discovery of a novel tandem pore potassium channel activated by volatile anesthetics.

He completed his anesthesia residency at UCSF and was honored with the Resident Teacher of the Year Award. As a resident, he developed a keen interest in anesthesia history and wrote two papers, one of which investigated Sir William Macewen's first attempts at oral tracheal intubation in the late 19th Century. He presented his second paper for the John Bullough Prize at Cambridge University on Dr. Chauncey Leake's development of divinyl oxide at UCSF in the early 1930s.

After residency, Mazurek joined Southern Arizona Anesthesia Services, PC, as a partner in private practice. He was elected Chair of Anesthesia at St. Mary's hospital in Tucson, Arizona, and where he subsequently served as Chief-of-Staff. His experiences led him to pursue graduate studies and certifications in leadership.

He obtained a Master's in Healthcare Administration with distinction at Colorado State University, Global, specializing in information technology and systems; Certified Physician Executive (CPE) certification through the American Association for Physician Leadership; and Fellow of the

American College of Healthcare Executives (FACHE) certification through the American College of Healthcare Executives.

With numerous appointments at multiple medical schools and CRNA programs, he has taught hundreds of students and has presented on a wide variety of topics, including leadership, professionalism, and peri-operative surgical care at national and local conferences.

After serving as Medical Director with Envision Physician Services and Sanford Health in Bemidji, Minnesota, he continues to teach, write, and pursue leadership education and research as an Assistant Clinical Professor in the Department of Anesthesia at the Yale School of Medicine.

ACKNOWLEDGMENTS

I would like to thank my wife, Kari, and daughter, Ariel. Their patience, love and support as I 'burned the midnight oil' made a difference and is appreciated. Many members of Central Valley Astronomers, Inc. (CVA) influenced me as I grew up in Fresno, California. Specifically, Garrett Wimer and Clarence Funk were mentors and groomed me as I became the youngest president of CVA in the early 1990s. When I was a student and lecturer at Fresno State, Dr. Steven White, Dr. John Donaldson, and Dr. Brandt Kehoe from the Physics Department provided opportunities for me to learn, teach, and grow.

At UCSF, Dr. C. Spencer Yost took me under his wing and offered years of support and gave me the opportunity to conduct research in anesthesia. He was instrumental in helping me in my career as a student and resident. I remain grateful. Dr. Merlin Larson, too, assisted me in my efforts as I studied interesting topics on the history of anesthesia as a resident. Dr. Ron Miller, former Chair of Anesthesia at UCSF, my program director, Dr. Mark Rosen, and Dr. James Sonner provided invaluable support throughout my residency.

My colleagues from Southern Arizona Anesthesia and St. Mary's Hospital, Drs. Karl Hekimian, Michael Hecht, Chris O'Neill, Herb McReynolds, Scott Berman, Amy Beiter, and Susan Thompson helped me immensely as I took on progressively difficult leadership roles. I would also like to thank Dr. Ronald Kaufman, former CMO of Tenet Healthcare, and Dr. Don Denmark, former CMO of Carondelet Health Network. I avoided many landmines thanks to their guidance. I would also like to thank my Vice-Chief at Sanford Bemidji Medical Center, Richard Hoff, CRNA, who led by example as a leader in anesthesia for nearly forty years practicing in rural northern Minnesota.

Thank you to my colleagues, Dr. Sean O'Dell, Dr. Benjamin Guslits, Dr. Joshua Bloomstone, Dr. Joe Loskove, and Mark Sechrist, MHA at Envision Physician Services who gave me opportunities to lead and participate on numerous committees. It was an honor to work with you.

Finally, I would like to thank Nancy Collins and Patricia George, editors of this book, for offering suggestions and guidance. This has been a great learning experience. I am humbled to have learned a lot about leadership from many great people and professional colleagues. Thank you again for your support.

STATEMENT OF PURPOSE, MISSION, AND FOCUS

One of the most difficult tasks physician leaders regularly face is managing and mitigating unprofessional physician conduct or complaints about physician behavior from patients, colleagues, nurses, and staff. Navigating the process effectively is usually a trial-by-fire exercise for most physicians who have just accepted a leadership position. My own leadership journey included learning how to investigate professional behavior issues, conduct meetings, and continue with follow-up, including discipline and peer support. I stumbled along the way and made mistakes. Having a roadmap with a variety of case examples would have helped me better manage disruptive behaviors. Newly appointed or elected physician leaders, especially, are nervous and uncomfortable confronting these issues with their colleagues. This book aims to assuage those concerns and instill confidence.

Also not being afraid to stand up for what you believe in while taking into account you could very well be wrong, or maybe there's another way to look at it — that things are not what they seem to be, and that everything is subjective.

—Surya Das

INTRODUCTION

As a medical student and trainee nearly 20 years ago, I heard the legendary stories of surgeons throwing scalpels, drinking on call, and engaging in blatant sexual harassment. Unfortunately, hospitals, colleagues, and others allowed this behavior to continue without disciplinary action. Excuses were parsed out by administrators who feared losing business from high-producing physicians. Consequently, these behaviors continued for decades.

The Joint Commission, recognizing the need for hospitals and medical staffs to intervene, released a statement on the consequences of disruptive behavior as a *Sentinel Event Alert* in Issue 40 on July 9, 2008. The message was clear: Disruptive behavior harmed patients and led to medical errors.

Physician leaders, including department chairs, presidents of medical staffs, Chief Medical Officers, and other appointed leaders and colleagues, often lack formal training or guidance on how to "manage" physicians engaged in unprofessional behavior. There are professional, personal, and legal pitfalls, and everyone engaged in the process is uncomfortable.

Over the past decade, my role as Chair of Anesthesia, Chief of Staff, Medical Director, and Chair of Professional Behavior Committees has given me the opportunity to conduct dozens of investigations of unprofessional and disruptive conduct from the mundane to the serious. This book offers practical advice and guidance on managing disruptive behavior with real-world case examples, in-depth discussion on the process, description and analysis of personal traits and disorders of disruptive physicians, and strategies to reduce the incidence of these behaviors.

> *All the world's a stage,*
> *And all the men and women merely players;*
> *They have their exits and their entrances*
> *And one man in his time plays many parts . . .*
> —*Shakespeare, As You Like It*

THE JOINT COMMISSION SENTINEL EVENT ALERT 40: BEHAVIORS THAT UNDERMINE A CULTURE OF SAFETY

Behaviors that undermine a culture of safety

Intimidating and disruptive behaviors can foster medical errors,[1,2,3] contribute to poor patient satisfaction and to preventable adverse outcomes,[1,4,5] increase the cost of care,[4,5] and cause qualified clinicians, administrators, and managers to seek new positions in more professional environments.[1,6] Safety and quality of patient care is dependent on teamwork, communication, and a collaborative work environment. To assure quality and to promote a culture of safety, health care organizations must address the problem of behaviors that threaten the performance of the health care team.

Intimidating and disruptive behaviors include overt actions such as verbal outbursts and physical threats, as well as passive activities such as refusing to perform assigned tasks or quietly exhibiting uncooperative attitudes during routine activities. Intimidating and disruptive behaviors are often manifested by health care professionals in positions of power. Such behaviors include reluctance or refusal to answer questions, return phone calls or pages; condescending language or voice intonation; and impatience with questions.[2] Overt and passive behaviors undermine team effectiveness and can compromise the safety of patients.[7,8,11] All intimidating and disruptive behaviors are unprofessional and should not be tolerated.

Intimidating and disruptive behaviors in health care organizations are not rare.[1,2,7,8,9] A survey on intimidation conducted by the Institute for Safe Medication Practices found that 40 percent of clinicians have kept quiet or remained passive during patient care events rather than question a known intimidator.[2,10] While most formal research centers on intimidating and disruptive behaviors among physicians and nurses, there is evidence that these behaviors occur among other health care professionals, such as pharmacists, therapists, and support staff, as well as among administrators.[1,2] Several surveys have found that most care providers have experienced or witnessed intimidating or disruptive behaviors.[1,2,8,12,13] These behaviors are not limited to one gender and occur during interactions within and across

1

disciplines.[1,2,7] Nor are such behaviors confined to the small number of individuals who habitually exhibit them.[2] It is likely that these individuals are not involved in the large majority of episodes of intimidating or disruptive behaviors. It is important that organizations recognize that it is the behaviors that threaten patient safety, irrespective of who engages in them.

The majority of health care professionals enter their chosen discipline for altruistic reasons and have a strong interest in caring for and helping other human beings. The preponderance of these individuals carry out their duties in a manner consistent with this idealism and maintain high levels of professionalism. The presence of intimidating and disruptive behaviors in an organization, however, erodes professional behavior and creates an unhealthy or even hostile work environment — one that is readily recognized by patients and their families. Health care organizations that ignore these behaviors also expose themselves to litigation from both employees and patients. Studies link patient complaints about unprofessional, disruptive behaviors and malpractice risk.[13,14,15] "Any behavior which impairs the health care team's ability to function well creates risk," says Gerald Hickson, M.D., associate dean for Clinical Affairs and director of the Center for Patient and Professional Advocacy at Vanderbilt University Medical Center. "If health care organizations encourage patients and families to speak up, their observations and complaints, if recorded and fed back to organizational leadership, can serve as part of a surveillance system to identify behaviors by members of the health care team that create unnecessary risk."

Root causes and contributing factors

There is a history of tolerance and indifference to intimidating and disruptive behaviors in health care.[10] Organizations that fail to address unprofessional behavior through formal systems are indirectly promoting it.[9,11] Intimidating and disruptive behavior stems from both individual and systemic factors.[4] The inherent stresses of dealing with high stakes, high emotion situations can contribute to occasional intimidating or disruptive behavior, particularly in the presence of factors such as fatigue. Individual care providers who exhibit characteristics such as self-centeredness, immaturity, or defensiveness can be more prone to unprofessional behavior.[8,11] They can lack interpersonal, coping or conflict management skills.

Systemic factors stem from the unique health care cultural environment, which is marked by pressures that include increased productivity demands, cost containment requirements, embedded hierarchies, and fear of or stress from litigation. These pressures can be further exacerbated by changes to or differences in the authority, autonomy, empowerment, and roles or values of professionals on the health care team,[5,7,16] as well as by the continual flux of daily changes in shifts, rotations, and interdepartmental support staff. This dynamic creates challenges for inter-professional communication and for the development of trust among team members.

Disruptive behaviors often go unreported, and therefore unaddressed, for a number of reasons. Fear of retaliation and the stigma associated with "blowing the whistle" on a colleague, as well as a general reluctance to confront an intimidator all contribute to underreporting of intimidating and/or disruptive behavior.[2,9,12,16] Additionally, staff within institutions often perceive that powerful, revenue-generating physicians are "let off the hook" for inappropriate behavior due to the perceived consequences of confronting them.[8,10,12,17] The American College of Physician Executives (ACPE) conducted a physician behavior survey and found that 38.9 percent of the respondents agreed that "physicians in my organization who generate high amounts of revenue are treated more leniently when it comes to behavior problems than those who bring in less revenue."[17]

Existing Joint Commission requirements

Effective January 1, 2009 for all accreditation programs, The Joint Commission has a new Leadership standard (LD.03.01.01)* that addresses disruptive and inappropriate behaviors in two of its elements of performance: Issue 40: Behaviors that undermine a culture of safety | Joint Commission http://www.jointcommission.org/SentinelEvents/SentinelEventAlert/sea_40.htm?print=yes[9/20/2010 11:54:55 AM]

> EP 4: The hospital/organization has a code of conduct that defines acceptable and disruptive and inappropriate behaviors.
> EP 5: Leaders create and implement a process for managing disruptive and inappropriate behaviors.

Effective Jan. 1, 2022, new workplace violence standards provide a framework to guide hospitals and critical access hospitals in defining workplace violence; developing strong workplace violence prevention systems; and developing a leadership structure, policies and procedures, reporting systems, post-incident strategies, training, and education to decrease workplace violence. The new requirements are located at Environment of Care standard EC.02.01.01 EP 17; Human Resources standard HR.01.05.03 EP 29; and LD.03.01.01 EP 9. In addition, EC.04.01.01 EPs 1 and 6 have been revised

In addition, standards in the Medical Staff chapter have been organized to follow six core competencies (see the introduction to MS.4) to be addressed in the credentialing process, including interpersonal skills and professionalism.

Other Joint Commission suggested actions

1. Educate all team members — both physicians and non-physician staff — on appropriate professional behavior defined by the organization's code of conduct. The code and education should emphasize respect. Include training in basic business etiquette (particularly phone skills) and people skills.[10, 18,19]

2. Hold all team members accountable for modeling desirable behaviors and enforce the code consistently and equitably among all staff regardless of seniority or clinical discipline in a positive fashion through reinforcement as well as punishment.[2,4,9,10,11]

3. Develop and implement policies and procedures/processes appropriate for the organization that address:

   a. "Zero tolerance" for intimidating and/or disruptive behaviors, especially the most egregious instances of disruptive behavior such as assault and other criminal acts. Incorporate the zero-tolerance policy into medical staff bylaws and employment agreements as well as administrative policies.

   b. Medical staff policies regarding intimidating and/or disruptive behaviors of physicians within a health care organization should be complementary and supportive of the policies that are present in the organization for non-physician staff.

   c. Reducing fear of intimidation or retribution and protecting those who report or cooperate in the investigation of intimidating, disruptive and other unprofessional behavior.[10,18] Non-retaliation clauses should be included in all policy statements that address disruptive behaviors.

    d. Responding to patients and/or their families who are involved in or witness intimidating and/or disruptive behaviors. The response should include hearing and empathizing with their concerns, thanking them for sharing those concerns, and apologizing.[11]

    e. How and when to begin disciplinary actions (such as suspension, termination, loss of clinical privileges, reports to professional licensure bodies).

4. Develop an organizational process for addressing intimidating and disruptive behaviors (LD.3.10 EP 5) that solicits and integrates substantial input from an inter-professional team including representation of medical and nursing staff, administrators, and other employees.[4,10,18]

5. Provide skills-based training and coaching for all leaders and managers in relationship-building and collaborative practice, including skills for giving feedback on unprofessional behavior, and conflict resolution.[4,7,10,11,17,20] Cultural assessment tools can also be used to measure whether or not attitudes change over time.

6. Develop and implement a system for assessing staff perceptions of the seriousness and extent of instances of unprofessional behaviors and the risk of harm to patients.[10,17,18]

7. Develop and implement a reporting/surveillance system (possibly anonymous) for detecting unprofessional behavior. Include ombuds services [20] and patient advocates,[2,11] both of which provide important feedback from patients and families who may experience intimidating or disruptive behavior from health professionals. Monitor system effectiveness through regular surveys, focus groups, peer and team member evaluations, or other methods.[10] Have multiple and specific strategies to learn whether intimidating or disruptive behaviors exist or recur, such as through direct inquiries at routine intervals with staff, supervisors, and peers.

8. Support surveillance with tiered, non-confrontational interventional strategies, starting with informal "cup of coffee" conversations directly addressing the problem and moving toward detailed action plans and progressive discipline if patterns persist.[4,5,10,11] These interventions should initially be non-adversarial in nature, with the focus

on building trust, placing accountability on, and rehabilitating the offending individual, and protecting patient safety.[4,5] Make use of mediators and conflict coaches when professional dispute resolution skills are needed.[4,7,14]

9. Conduct all interventions within the context of an organizational commitment to the health and well-being of all staff,[11] with adequate resources to support individuals whose behavior is caused or influenced by physical or mental health pathologies.

10. Encourage inter-professional dialogues across a variety of forums as a proactive way of addressing ongoing conflicts, overcoming them, and moving forward through improved collaboration and communication.[1,2,4,10]

11. Document all attempts to address intimidating and disruptive behaviors.[18]

REFERENCES

1. Rosenstein, AH, O'Daniel, M: Disruptive behavior and clinical outcomes: Perceptions of nurses and physicians. *American Journal of Nursing*, 2005, 105,1,54-64

2. Institute for Safe Medication Practices: Survey on workplace intimidation. 2003. Available online: https://ismp.org/Survey/surveyresults/Survey0311.asp (accessed April 14, 2008)

3. Morrissey J: Encyclopedia of errors; Growing database of medication errors allows hospitals to compare their track records with facilities nationwide in a nonpunitive setting. *Modern Healthcare*, March 24, 2003, 33(12):40,42

4. Gerardi, D: Effective strategies for addressing "disruptive" behavior: Moving from avoidance to engagement. Medical Group Issue 40: Behaviors that undermine a culture of safety | Joint Commission http://www.jointcommission.org/SentinelEvents/SentinelEventAlert/sea_40.htm?print=yes[9/20/2010 11:54:55 AM] Management Association Webcast, 2007; and Gerardi, D: Creating Cultures of Engagement: Effective Strategies for Addressing Conflict and "Disruptive" Behavior. Arizona Hospital Association Annual Patient Safety Forum, 2008

5. Ransom, SB, and Neff, KE, et al: *Enhancing physician performance.* American College of Physician Executives, Tampa, Fla., 2000, chapter 4, p.45-72

6. Rosenstein, A, et al: Disruptive physician behavior contributes to nursing shortage: Study links bad behavior by doctors to nurses leaving the profession. *Physician Executive,* November/December 2002, 28(6):8-11. Available online: http://findarticles.com/p/articles/mi_m0843/is_6_28/ai_94590407 (accessed April 14, 2008)

7. Gerardi, D: The Emerging Culture of Health Care: Improving End-of-Life Care through Collaboration and Conflict Engagement Among Health Care Professionals. Ohio State Journal on Dispute Resolution, 2007, 23(1):105-142

8. Weber, DO: Poll results: Doctors' disruptive behavior disturbs physician leaders. *Physician Executive*, September/October 2004, 30(5):6-14

9. Leape, LL and Fromson, JA: Problem doctors: Is there a system-level solution? *Annals of Internal Medicine*, 2006, 144:107- 155

10. Porto, G and Lauve, R: Disruptive clinical behavior: A persistent threat to patient safety. *Patient Safety and Quality Healthcare*, July/August 2006. Available online: http://www.psqh.com/julaug06/disruptive.html (accessed April 14, 2008)

11. Hickson, GB: A complementary approach to promoting professionalism: Identifying, measuring, and addressing unprofessional behaviors. *Academic Medicine*, November 2007, 82(11):1040-1048

12. Rosenstein, AH: Nurse-physician relationships: Impact on nurse satisfaction and retention. *American Journal of Nursing*, 2002, 102(6):26-34

13. Hickson GB, et al: Patient complaints and malpractice risk. Journal of the American Medical Association, 2002, 287:2951-7

14. Hickson GB, et al; Patient complaints and malpractice risk in a regional healthcare center. *Southern Medical Journal*, August 2007, 100(8):791-6

15. Stelfox HT, Ghandi TK, Orav J, Gustafson ML: The relation of patient satisfaction with complaints against physicians, risk management episodes, and malpractice lawsuits. *American Journal of Medicine*, 2005, 118(10):1126-33

16. Gerardi, D: The culture of health care: How professional and organizational cultures impact conflict management. *Georgia Law Review*, 2005, 21(4):857-890

17. Keogh, T and Martin, W: Managing unmanageable physicians. *Physician Executive*, September/October 2004, 18-22

18. ECRI Institute: *Disruptive practitioner behavior report*, June 2006. Available for purchase online: http://www.ecri.org/Press/Pages/Free_Report_Behavior.aspx (accessed April 14, 2008)

19. Kahn, MW: Etiquette-based medicine. *New England Journal of Medicine*, May 8, 2008, 358; 19:1988-1989

20. Marshall, P and Robson, R: Preventing and managing conflict: Vital pieces in the patient safety puzzle. *Healthcare Quarterly*, October 2005, 8:39

CHAPTER 1

History of Disruptive Behavior

"History is a relentless master. It has no present, only the past rushing into the future. To try to hold fast is to be swept aside."

– JOHN F. KENNEDY

ALTHOUGH "DISRUPTIVE PHYSICIAN BEHAVIOR" IS a relatively new term that first appeared in the literature in 1995,[1] it is not a new concept. In 1875, *The New York Times* published an article titled "Pugnacious Physicians." After an Academy of Medicine meeting, several physicians were charged with threatening personal assault to each other through the use of "deadly weapons."

Three days after President Garfield was shot on July 2, 1881, *The New York Times* published an article titled "Physicians Quarreling" detailing the behavior of two physicians who were treating the wounded president in an adjacent room. One physician called the other a liar, and the accused physician quickly jumped to his feet with "hostile intent." No doubt, these stories captivated the public's attention but also highlighted the lack of what we today call professionalism.

One must appreciate that medical education and training in the United States in the late 1800s and early 1900s was a for-profit enterprise that produced many poorly trained physicians. With no educational standards, anyone with the economic means could become a physician. That changed after the Flexner Report was released in 1910.[2] The report, written by Abraham Flexner for the Carnegie Foundation, found a majority of medical schools were providing substandard education and training. In fact, nearly 30% of medical schools closed as a result of Flexner's findings and recommendations.

It is easy to imagine some of these physicians were guilty of performing unnecessary surgeries and taking advantage of their status. The idea of poorly trained physicians preying on an ignorant public for personal gain brought forth a necessary change in how doctors were trained. In essence, this was the first step in recognizing the need for physicians to become professionals in the true sense of the word.

Throughout most of the 20th century, disruptive physician behavior was tolerated and became an engrained part of the "culture of medicine." Ten years prior to the Joint Commission's *Sentinel Alert 40*, the Council on Ethical and Judicial Affairs presented a report on "Physicians with Disruptive Behavior" to a committee of the American Medical Association. The report provided definitions, interventions, and recommendations.

Recognizing a problem is different from solving a problem. Despite widespread recognition and awareness, disruptive physician behaviors continue to negatively affect patient care and the work environment. Our healthcare system, hospitals, and licensing and governing boards lack a standardized, consistent, universally recognized definition of disruptive behavior, code of conduct, and process for managing disruptive physicians.

REFERENCES

1. Veltman L. The Disruptive Physician: The Risk Manager's Role. *Journal of Healthcare Risk Management.* 1995;15:11–16.
2. Flexner A. *Medical Education in the United States and Canada.* Boston: Merrymount Press; 1910.

CHAPTER 2

Definition of Disruptive Behavior

*You cannot become a peacemaker without
communication. Silence is a passive-aggressive grenade
thrown by insecure people that want war, but they
do not want the accountability of starting it.*

– SHANNON ALDER

I N ITS SIMPLEST TERMS, DISRUPTIVE behavior is *any* behavior or action that interrupts or compromises the professional work environment, workflow, or patient care. The Joint Commission's Alert clearly defines and describes disruptive behaviors that impact patient safety and the work environment. The American Medical Association, in their code of medical ethics, defines disruptive behavior as "personal conduct, whether verbal or physical, that negatively affects or that potentially may affect patient care."[1]

Until 2009, egregious behaviors often were the only precipitating event leading to disciplinary action, and many healthcare organizations did not consistently enforce clearly defined expectations, rules, and codes of conduct. Fortunately, over the past decade, most, if not all, healthcare organizations have adopted formal codes of conduct and processes to address disruptive behaviors.

A recent concern for some physician staff leaders and medical staff organizations is the misuse of the term "disruptive." Disagreeing with and engaging in constructive criticism of C-suite executives or colleagues is not disruptive behavior. Choosing not to participate or volunteer on a committee is not disruptive behavior. Huntoon wrote a brief editorial published in the *Journal of American Physicians and Surgeons* specifically addressing the possibility of gross overreach in defining disruptive physician behavior.[2]

To avoid misinterpretation and misuse, codes of conduct must include clear, well-defined examples of conduct and expectations. Without clear definitions, a code of conduct can be weaponized by administrators or staff members who deliberately report violations or minor infractions that are not explicitly defined in the conduct document.

As an example, a code of conduct that includes in its definition of disruptive behaviors "and any other behavior not delineated but deemed inappropriate by the Medical Executive Committee, Chief of Staff, or CEO" is a potential legal landmine and a setup for medical staff conflict.

Petrovic and Scholl posit that one of the reasons disruptive behavior continues to be a problem is the plurality of terms used to define disruptive behavior.[3] I agree. *The lack of a single definition hinders validated research on causes and effective interventions.*

Despite these challenges, Petrovic and Scholl's research identified the frequency of commonly used terms in their literature search (Table 1).[3]

TABLE 1. Commonly Used Terms for Disruptive Behavior

Disruptive Behavior Term	Total Count
Sexual harassment	27
Intimidation	24
Throwing	16
Physical abuse	14
Physical threats	14
Verbal abuse	13
Condescension	12
Yelling	11
Physical behavior negatively impacting patient care	10
Verbal behavior negatively impacting patient care	10
Profanity, swearing, foul language	9

Interestingly, most of these behaviors are aggressive, disruptive, and in some cases, criminal. Despite the continued challenge of identifying a single, unifying definition, it is possible and practical to use broad definitions in a code of conduct.

TYPES OF PHYSICIAN DISRUPTIVE BEHAVIORS

Disruptive behaviors can be categorized as passive, passive-aggressive, and aggressive. Categorizing the behavior by type helps leaders approach an investigation and intervention. Although there are clear lines of definition between aggressive and passive-aggressive, the categories blur between passive-aggressive and passive behaviors. Examples of the various types of disruptive behaviors are provided in Table 2.

TABLE 2. Categories of Disruptive Behaviors

Passive	Passive-Aggressive	Aggressive
• Chronic tardiness • Incomplete charting • Failing to respond to calls/pages • Avoidant behavior • Ignoring e-mails, texts • Ignoring requests/consults	• Sarcasm • Veiled threats • Backhanded compliments • Inappropriate charting • Derogatory comments • Undermining or constant questioning of another physician's care • Inappropriate jokes • Demeaning comments about colleagues, hospital, or staff • Discussing unfounded rumors and gossip	• Physical aggression • Yelling/Screaming • Throwing objects or instruments • Sexual harassment/assault • Bullying • Intimidating or threatening others • Consistent use of profane language

Passive Disruptive Behaviors

Physicians who demonstrate passive disruptive behaviors present a unique challenge. For example, physicians who do not routinely complete charts or answer e-mails may be so far behind in their work that they feel overwhelmed and simply give up. As a result, the backlog of charts or unanswered e-mails continues to grow until it becomes an unmanageable problem that negatively impacts patient care or the finances of the hospital or clinic. The behaviors are not necessarily malicious, although this is not always the case. When a physician purposefully decides not to answer calls or complete charts, the physician is behaving in a passive-aggressive manner.

This is one of the reasons the distinction between passive and passive-aggressive behavior is difficult to state clearly. Is the physician intentionally engaged in the behavior, or is it simply the result of poor time management or laziness? In the case studies presented in Chapter 7, I discuss the various types of passive behaviors and offer suggestions for managing them.

Passive-Aggressive Behaviors

Because passive-aggressive behaviors are widespread in our communities, families, schools, and workplaces, we often overlook them as disruptive unless they are obvious or frequent. People use passive-aggressive behavior for several reasons.[4] For example, we are taught to preserve and model "good" behavior; expressed anger is considered "uncivilized." However, expressing anger through hostility in the form of passive-aggressive behavior is more socially acceptable. It is easier to engage in passive-aggressive behaviors than practice the "soft skills" that must be learned and that require emotional management and assertiveness.

Passive-aggressive behavior is also easily rationalized. For example, a parent asks a child to clean her room, and the child refuses or procrastinates. When the parent becomes agitated, the child, recognizing the rising emotional tension, responds, "I was doing my homework first!" Instead of accepting responsibility, the child manipulates the situation and plays the victim. Obviously, doing homework is the more important task, and the child is leveraging this knowledge in a power struggle.

Another passive-aggressive tactic is seeking revenge. An employee who feels overworked and unappreciated calls in sick a couple of days to delay the completion of a critical project. The team misses the project deadline, and the manager is passed over for a promotion due to the delays. The employee knew the absence would cause the team, and ultimately their boss, to fail.

The hierarchical healthcare organization environment, unfortunately, is ripe with opportunity for sarcastic comments, put-downs, inappropriate jokes, and other passive-aggressive behaviors. The power dynamic is palpable and culturally acknowledged, and exacerbates the impact of these behaviors on subordinates and other team members. Unchecked, passive-aggressive behaviors lead to lower staff morale, lower productivity, higher staff turnover, and ultimately, compromised patient care and medical errors.

Aggressive Behaviors

Aggression is the most common type of behavior reported in the legendary stories of egregious behaviors. Physical assault, sexual assault, sexual harassment, threats, bullying, and other intimidating behaviors are easy to identify. These types of behaviors are as serious as they sound, and depending on the situation, can lead to even more harm for all parties if mishandled. Therefore, it is imperative to know exactly what to do in each situation.

Aggressive behaviors that pose an immediate threat and risk need to be managed quickly and appropriately, and the intervention needs to be swift and decisive. In the exceedingly rare event that the situation is dire, calling law enforcement may be the correct decision.

In the past 20 years, workplace bullying in general has increased. It is not a new phenomenon, however, and research on workplace bullying is relatively recent — the first paper on bullying in the workplace was published in 1990.[5] Medical training occurs within a hierarchy conducive to workplace bullying. Because there are numerous subordinates, the number of opportunities for those in positions of power and authority to engage in bullying behavior is high.

CONSEQUENCES OF DISRUPTIVE BEHAVIOR

Consequences of disruptive behavior include low morale, high turnover, and compromised care, which all come with a high cost.

High Turnover and Low Morale

According to the 2019 National Healthcare Retention & RN Staffing Report, published by Nursing Solutions, Inc., the turnover rate for hospitals' bedside nurses has grown to 17.2%. Each percent change in nurse turnover will cost (or save) the average hospital an additional $328,400. The average turnover costs result in hospitals losing $4.4 million to $6.9 million each year. The report also determined it takes an average of 85 days to fill a nursing position (three months or more for a specialized nursing position), costing about $82,000 (not counting the costs associated with overtime work by other nurses, locums, and time to onboard and train the new nurse).[6]

Several studies from the late 1980s and 1990s revealed high rates of verbal abuse of staff nurses by physicians; nearly 90% of nurses reported verbal abuse by a physician over the course of a year.[7,8,9] Widespread prevalence and tolerance of disruptive behaviors is associated with higher levels of anxiety, psychosomatic symptoms, fatigue, absenteeism, and the inclination to change jobs or leave the nursing profession.[10,11] The consequences of these behaviors lead to medical errors, delayed care, and decreased morale.

Staff morale and employee satisfaction and performance are inextricably intertwined.[12] Although many factors influence morale, a culture that allows disrespect and disruptive behavior has a profound impact. Nurses and physicians alike often train in a highly dysfunctional culture that allows humiliating behavior and demeaning treatment of trainees, students, and residents.[13] A 1990 *JAMA* article reported on a survey of the incidence, severity, and significance of medical student abuse. Approximately 46.4% of all respondents stated that they had been abused at some time while enrolled in medical school, with 80.6% of senior medical students reporting being abused by their senior year.[14]

Although I experienced bullying while on my pediatrics rotation during my third year of medical school, I never reported my experience. Assigned to a team for the duration of the clerkship meant I had a longitudinal experience with a chief resident, two junior residents, and two interns. I felt, as many third-year clerks do, the least-educated and least-capable member of the team. Unfortunately, this pecking order exists due to the nature of our training.

One of the interns did not match and had to find an internship in the famous "scramble" whereby unmatched medical students can find places with unfilled residency positions. I quickly realized why this intern failed to match. His sarcastic, acrid attitude toward being an intern in a transitional program that he did not want was obvious. Within a couple of days, while we were discussing a patient in private, he referred to me as "pond scum." My immediate reaction, knowing what type of person he was, was to simply ignore it. His berating continued here and there, at odd times, but I did not report it at the time; I waited until I was finished with my rotation and had earned my marks and comments.

There were several reasons I did not want to report the bullying behavior. First, I did not want to be perceived as someone who "rocked the boat." I intuitively knew it would lead to interviews, inquiries, reports, monitoring, and meetings. *The consequences of reporting the behavior would distract me from my education more than living with the behavior would.*

Second, I knew the name-calling was more reflective of him than it was of me. I had enough self-esteem to know that, as a hard-working medical student at UCSF, I certainly was not "pond scum."

Third, I did not want it to affect my marks on the rotation. Comments from the rotations are inserted, sometimes verbatim, into our Dean's Letter when we apply for residency programs. The last thing I needed was an asterisk or poor comment.

Finally, the rotation length had a quick end date. I could simply navigate through the situation for eight weeks and move on.

Despite efforts to reduce medical student bullying and abuse, it continues.[15] A recent study explored medical students' barriers to reporting mistreatment during clerkships. Several themes emerged from the study:

1. Fear of reprisal even in the setting of anonymity.
2. Perception that mistreatment is part of medical culture.
3. Difficulty reporting subtle forms of mistreatment.
4. Incident not important enough to report.
5. Damage to the student-teacher relationship.
6. Cumbersome process.
7. Empathy with the source of mistreatment.

I must emphasize there is a lot at stake for students in any professional program. These barriers to reporting are barriers in our progress to alleviate and eliminate abuse. Some of these themes will be discussed further in the case studies.

Nurses, too, experience bullying and mistreatment in school and as new graduates. Nurse bullying even has a term: "eating our young." Nearly 78% of students experience bullying in nursing school, and nearly 60% of nurse managers, directors, and executives experience bullying in the workplace; 26% consider the bullying "severe."[15] Nurses often feel that abuse and bullying are just part of the culture of medicine.[16]

Medical and nursing school and training programs continue to have issues with bullying and mistreatment. This culture reduces the capacity for resilience, endurance, and empathy. It is the antithesis of why many of us chose a career in medicine. We have a moral obligation to foster a caring environment not only for our patients but for ourselves and our colleagues. Medical and nursing schools must prioritize a positive learning environment that has zero tolerance for bullying behaviors and mistreatment.

Patient Safety

On December 1, 1999, the Institute of Medicine released *To Err is Human: Building a Safer Health System.* The startling truth about the American healthcare system was laid bare: An estimated 44,000 to 98,000 people die annually from medical errors.[17] We suffered from hubris. Despite the technological, pharmacologic, and research-driven advances in healthcare, we had a lot of work to do to fix a broken system. As much as systems processes and human errors are to blame for medical errors leading to increased morbidity and mortality, a tolerance of unprofessional behavior and poor communication was and continues to be a contributing, preventable factor.

Ineffective communication or belittling can directly impact patient care. Imagine the following vignette.

Dr. B is the night house officer, and after a day of seeing consults and rounding, goes to her call room for a brief rest. Eyes closed; the pager goes off five minutes later: *Medication order question on patient in Room 314. Becky—4569.*

Dr. B ignores the pager, places it back on the nightstand, and falls asleep. Fifteen minutes later, the same page is repeated. Frustrated and angry, Dr. B calls Becky at that extension and as Becky picks up the phone, Dr. B states, "I thought my orders are pretty clear. What do you want?" Becky replies, "The patient has an allergy to dilaudid and she is in pain. All you ordered was dilaudid from the order set. Can I give something else?"

Dr. B replies, "You know, that is the problem with this hospital. No one even bothers to see or ask what the patient means when they say they have an allergy to a medication. I spoke with the patient, and she said it made her feel dizzy. She doesn't get a rash, hives, or anything else to suggest she has an allergy, so go ahead and give the patient some dilaudid."

The nurse, a little shaken, says, "Well, pharmacy won't release it if it states she has an allergy to it." Dr. B, now angry, yells, "I said you can give the dilaudid!" and slams the phone down. The nurse reports this to the charge RN, and a formal complaint is filed with the residency program director.

I have witnessed nurses tell other nurses not to page a physician with a question because the physician does not like to get paged after a certain time in the afternoon or during clinic. I have intervened on a few of these occasions and contacted the physicians myself so the nurses could get clarity or have relevant questions answered. I cannot think of one good reason why a physician can justify this type of behavior. We have a responsibility to be available, when responsible, for questions or concerns about our patients. Capriciously setting up barriers combined with bad attitudes can lead to disaster.

In the scenario above, the patient did not receive pain medication in a timely manner, and the physician could have *kindly* picked up the phone and answered the page the first time —eliminating the need for another page. Nothing constructive emerged from the atmosphere of hostility the physician created. Safe patient care is only possible in a respectful environment with accurate, timely communication.

Economic Impact

The economic impact of poor physician conduct includes all aspects of care. Conduct that leads to poor outcomes increases costs through unexpected care or settled lawsuits. Turnover, as previously discussed, increases costs. A toxic work environment decreases staff productivity through absenteeism or the lack of communication leading to inefficiencies in care. Building service lines and recruiting new physicians is challenging if prospective physicians discover major problems with one of the future partners during the interview process. In aggregate, the total economic impact can easily approach seven figures annually.

A former CMO of mine successfully quantified the total economic impact of a physician who continually engaged in disruptive behavior. Several employees had quit the year prior, so estimating the cost of turnover was possible. The staff departures decreased productivity as well. Once the business case was made to intervene, the physician was finally terminated. One year later, productivity and revenue increased. The classic perception of the "high-earning" physician as an untouchable source of revenue is nothing more than an Achilles' Heel in the long run.

Non-Action Risks

The risks of non-action can lead to costly lawsuits, tarnished reputation, increased patient morbidity and mortality, continued cultural erosion, and lack of trust in the organization. Non-action is equivalent to maintaining the status quo and continued double-standard treatment of physicians vs. non-physicians. Non-action is a guaranteed path to failure, and it is no longer an option.

In late March 2021, a prominent university agreed to a record $1.1 billion settlement to nearly 750 women who were subject to abuse and inappropriate conduct by an OB/GYN physician who worked in the student health center for nearly three decades. Despite reports of abuse and allegations of misconduct more than 20 years ago, the university did nothing. One of the motives for inaction is the fear of loss of prominent donors and reputational harm. It is difficult for an institution to walk backward from the consequences of its inaction and provide any reasonable justification. Knowing something and doing nothing is complicity.

REFERENCES

1. American Medical Association. AMA Code of Medical Ethics. www.ama-assn.org/delivering-care/ethics/code-medical-ethics-overview.

2. Huntoon L. The Insulting Physician "Code of Conduct." *Journal of American Physicians and Surgeons*.2008;13(1):2–4.

3. Petrovic M and School A. Why We Need a Single Definition of Disruptive Behavior. *Cureus*. 2018;10(3): E2339.

4. Whitson S. 7 Reasons Why People Use Passive Aggressive Behavior. *Psychology Today*. March 16, 2104. www.psychologytoday.com/us/blog/passive-aggressive-diaries/201403/7-reasons-why-people-use-passive-aggressive-behavior.

5. Leymann H. Mobbing and Psychological Terror at Workplaces. *Violence and Victims*. 1990;5(2):119–126.

6. Shaffer F, Curtin L. Nurse Turnover: Understand It, Reduce It. *American Nurse*. August 10, 2020. www.myamericannurse.com/nurse-turnover-understand-it-reduce-it.

7. Cox H. Verbal Abuse in Nursing: Report of a Study. *Nursing Management*. 1987;22(3):72–76.

8. Chung M, Thang C, Vermillion M, Fried J, Uijtdehaage S. Exploring Medical Students' Barriers to Reporting Mistreatment During Clerkships: A Qualitative Study. *Medical Education Online*.2018;23(1):1478170. Published online May 31, 2018.

9. Diaz A, McMillin J. A Definition and Description of Nurse Abuse. *Western Journal of Nursing Research*.1991;13(1):97–109.

10. Mandario M, Berkey N. Verbal Abuse of Staff Nurses by Physicians. *Journal of Professional Nursing*. 1997;13(1):48–55.

11. Rosenstein A, Russell H, Lauve R. Disruptive Physician Behavior Contributes to Nursing Shortage. *The Physician Executive*. 2002; 28(6):8–11.

12. Osho G, Ashe C, Wickramatunge J. Correlation of Morale, Productivity, and Profit in Organizations. *National Social Science Journal*. 2006:26(1):108–115.

13. Leape L, Shore M, Dienstag J, et al. A Culture of Respect, Part 1: The Nature and Causes of Disrespectful Behavior by Physicians. *Academic Medicine*.2012;87(7):845–852.

14. Mavis B, Sousa A, Lipscomb W, et. al. Learning About Medical Student Mistreatment From Responses to the Medical School Graduation Questionnaire. *Academic Medicine*. 2014;89(5): 705–709.

15. Silver H & Glicken A. Medical Student Abuse: Incidence, Severity, and Significance. *JAMA*. 1990;263:527–532.

16. Edmonson C. & Zelonka C. Our Own Worst Enemies: The Nurse Bullying Epidemic. *Nursing Administration Quarterly*. 2019;43(3):274–279.

17. Institute of Medicine Committee on Quality of Health Care in America. *To Err Is Human: Building a Safer Health System*. Washington, DC: National Academies Press; 2000.

CHAPTER 3

Codes of Conduct, Bylaws, and Committees

You are always responsible for how you act, no matter how you feel.

– Robert Tew

I N 1918, THE AMERICAN COLLEGE of Surgeons created the first formal medical staff organization (MSO) in response to problems of that era — unnecessary surgeries and fee-splitting — and to prevent unqualified physicians from performing surgery.

It is important to note that early in the 20th century, formally measuring quality outcomes was non-existent. The original intent for the creation of an MSO was quality control through a group of peer physicians, and the MSO's primary purpose was to hold physicians collectively accountable for patient safety and clinical performance.[1]

The role of the MSO has not changed dramatically, but after the Joint Commission report was published in 2008, medical staffs and hospitals were responsible for creating codes of conduct and formal processes to reduce disruptive professional behaviors. It has been well over a decade since the report, and most, if not all, hospitals have a code of conduct or similar document. As part of the onboarding process, most physicians must acknowledge receiving and reading the code of conduct with a formal signature. Ensuring that new and present members of the medical staff are aware of the code of conduct is the first step in preventing conduct concerns. Signed copies are legal documents that protect the medical staff and hospital.

While the code of conduct may be a separate document, reporting, investigating, and managing professional behavior issues is usually a part of the medical staff bylaws, and courts in more than 20 states have held that the bylaws are a contract between the hospital and its physicians.[2]

The bylaws provide the roadmap for medical staff governance, patient care, peer review, credentialing, and privileging. If you are a new department chair, ask for a copy of the bylaws and read them thoroughly. Although tedious to read, it is a legal document and adherence to the due processes and procedures in the bylaws is expected. Adherence can help you avoid many of the legal pitfalls discussed later.

The process for reporting and investigating conduct complaints is different at each hospital or healthcare organization. Some hospitals recently implemented anonymous reporting systems that allow anyone in the organization to report a safety or conduct concern. As part of an effort toward high reliability, having the capacity to report even the most trivial concerns gives the organization a chance to prevent small problems from having a larger impact if these concerns are not addressed — including problems with professional behavior.

Another structure is a formal reporting system that uses nurse managers who report to department chairs. This is a common process, and from a medical staff governance perspective, it makes sense. The department chair is often a peer of the physician and likely works with or knows the physician in some capacity. There is familiarity, and while this can be an advantage, it can also be a disadvantage if the behavior continues.

Some hospitals grant authority to the Chief Medical Officer (CMO) to receive and investigate complaints. And in some settings, there is a hybrid system whereby department chairs process most complaints; if there are continued problems, the CMO or Chief of Staff intervenes. Regardless of the process, ensure you understand the chain of reporting and proper process. Lack of adherence to the policies, bylaws, or any other lapse increases legal risk.

The Appendix includes examples of code of conduct policies written by two different healthcare organizations. I renamed and reworded, when necessary, to keep the organizations anonymous. The first example is from an academic organization with an employed physician staff, and the second is from a healthcare system composed of a mixed, independent medical staff with private practice physicians.

Effective conduct policies define behavior and put forth professional expectations. Good bylaws and processes define who is responsible, how the conduct policy will be enforced, consequences, and the procedures and processes for fair hearings. If you find glaring lapses in your current policies or bylaws, seek feedback. In some cases, the bylaws or conduct code may need revision.

REFERENCES

1. Williams K. The Quandary of the Hospital Administrator in Dealing with the Medical Malpractice Problem. *Nebraska Law Review.* 1976;55(3):401–416.
2. Anesthesia Business Consultants. Your Other Hospital Contracts the Medical Staff Bylaws. www.anesthesiallc.com/publications/anesthesia-provider-news-ealerts/382-your-other-hospital-contracts-the-medical-staff-bylaws.

CHAPTER 4

Know Yourself: Your Emotional Intelligence Quotient (EIQ) and Behavior

*"He who knows others is wise; he who
knows himself is enlightened."*

– Lao Tzu

THE TERM "EMOTIONAL INTELLIGENCE" (EQ) first appeared in the mid-1960s.[1] In 1995, Daniel Goleman published his best-selling book *Emotional Intelligence: Why It Can Matter More Than IQ*. Emotional intelligence (EI) and the emotional intelligence quotient (EIQ) is an array of personality traits, behaviors, and characteristics that drive relationship behaviors. Those who score high on the EIQ scale are more successful at work, have better job performance, and are, for the most part, more effective leaders.[2]

Peter Salovey and John Mayer define emotional intelligence as "the ability to monitor one's own and other people's emotions, to discriminate between different emotions and label them appropriately, and to use emotional information to guide thinking and behavior." [3] The concept can further be broken down into four abilities: perceiving, using, understanding, and managing emotions.

Despite the challenges in defining emotional intelligence, understanding the concepts and theories can be useful for physician leaders in managing professional behavior. Disagreement about the definition of EI has led to the creation of different EI models: Ability Model, Mixed Model, and Trait Model.

The **Ability Model** views emotions as sources of information that can be useful on helping one evaluate and navigate a complex social environment.

Perceiving emotions is the ability to detect and decipher emotions in faces, body language, context, and situation. Using this information, we can respond accordingly to our environment within the context of our own emotional response. The result is an amalgam of emotional inputs, responses, and internal management and regulation.

The **Mixed Model** was introduced by Daniel Goleman in an article in the *Harvard Business Review* in 1998.[4] Goleman outlines five EI constructs[2]:

1. *Self-awareness* — being aware of our own emotions, strengths, weaknesses, and their impact on others.
2. *Self-regulation* — controlling our disruptive emotions and adapting to our environment.
3. *Social-skill* — managing our relationships with others.
4. *Empathy* — considering other people's emotions.
5. *Motivation* — having an awareness of what motivates others.

Figure 1 provides a snapshot of the EI concepts and how they relate to each other within the context of the individual and the social environment.

An underlying theme in EI is the capacity for empathy. Individuals who have the capacity to understand another individual's emotional state and point of view are at a distinct advantage socially if they can use this information to positively influence behavior or outcomes.

Goleman argues that within each of these five constructs are emotional competencies that can be learned. In other words, EI is not an innate ability but a learned capability. However, individuals are, he contends, born with a general EI that determines their potential for learning emotional competencies.[4]

Importantly, there are validated tools to measure EI using the Ability Model. The Emotional Competence Inventory was created in 1999, and in 2007, the Emotional and Social Competence Inventory (ESCI) was developed. The ESCI provides a comprehensive report on an individual's EI based on personal responses and other raters who participate in the evaluation. Rather than rely solely on self-reported answers, the results incorporate perspectives from managers, peers, customers, and anyone else who regularly interacts with the individual.

The **Trait Model** is unique, as this proposed model incorporates personality into the framework of EI. Trait EI is "a constellation of emotional

		Recognition	Regulation
Personal Competence		**Self-Awareness** ✓ Self-confidence ✓ Awareness of your emotional state ✓ Recognizing how your behavior impacts others ✓ Paying attention to how others influence your emotional state	**Self-Management** ✓ Getting along well with others ✓ Handling conflict effectively ✓ Clearly expressing ideas and information ✓ Using sensitivity to another person's feelings (empathy) to manage interactions successfully
Social Competence		**Social Awareness** ✓ Picking up on the mood in the room ✓ Caring what others are going through ✓ Hearing what the other person is "really" saying	**Relationship Management** ✓ Getting along well with others ✓ Handling conflict effectively ✓ Clearly expressing ideas/information ✓ Using sensitivity to another person's feelings (empathy) to manage interactions successfully

FIGURE 1. Emotional Intelligence Competencies

self-perceptions located at the lower levels of personality."[5] A main component of the Trait Model is the idea that EI is a personality trait, not necessarily subject to alteration. An advantage of this model is the appreciation of personality traits on EI and EIQ.

There is inherent value in knowing your own EIQ or being aware of the concepts of EIQ. This level of deeper awareness will make your leadership journey a lot more pleasant during difficult conversations. Specific behaviors will give you an edge. Active listening will help you better understand someone else's perspective. Acknowledging their emotional response and feelings about a situation gives you power. These two behaviors combined with positive action and consistent follow-through create trust.

REFERENCES

1. Beldoch M, Davitz J. *The Communication of Emotional Meaning.* Westport, CT: Greenwood Press; 1976.
2. Goleman D. *Emotional Intelligence.* New York: Random House; 1995.

3. Mayer JD, Salovey P. What Is Emotional Intelligence? In P. Salovey & D. Sluyter (eds). *Emotional Development and Emotional Intelligence: Implications for Educators.* (pp. 3–31). New York: Basic Books;1997.

4. Bayaz R, Goleman D, Rhee K. Clustering Competence in Emotional Intelligence: Insights from the Emotional Competence Inventory (ECI). In Baor-On R & Parker J (eds.). *Handbook of Emotional Intelligence.* (pp. 343–362). San Francisco: Jossey-Bass;2000.

5. Petrides KV, Furnham A, and Mavroveli S. Trait Emotional Intelligence: Moving Forward in the Field of EI. In G Matthews, M Zeidner, & RD Roberts (eds.) *The Science of Emotional Intelligence: Knowns and Unknowns.* (pp. 288–304). Oxford: Oxford University Press;2007.

CHAPTER 5

Determining Your Leadership Style

Corporate culture matters. How management chooses to treat its people impacts everything — for better or for worse.

– SIMON SINEK

Before you are a leader, success is all about growing yourself. When you become a leader, success is all about growing others.

– JACK WELCH

LEADERSHIP SKILLS ARE NOT FORMALLY taught in medical school. Getting into medical school is an individual effort, and academic success, scores on the MCAT, and further testing through the USMLE Step exams largely determine whether a student can successfully navigate the process of becoming a physician. It is *mostly* an academic exercise. It remains a solid truth that the hardest part of becoming a physician is simply getting into medical school. Once in, the system is designed for students to succeed.

The best opportunity to lead during the training process is during residency when the young physician leads teams of medical students, interns, and junior residents. I vividly recall senior residents who did a great job and, conversely, those who did not. Many residency programs are recognizing the need to address the gap in leadership training as medical care is transforming into "care team models" comprised of attendings, nurse practitioners, physician assistants, and a variety of other support positions.

Medical training mirrors military leadership and training, so authority and leadership are based on an individual's training status as they progress. Academic success and excellent clinical skills are not necessarily strong foundations for leadership and effective team management. This does not mean physicians in general are not good leaders, but most young physicians lack the experience and training to lead because that is not the focus of medical training. With no formal program, young physicians who are motivated to learn how to lead more effectively often have to carve out this path on their own through mentors, formal coursework, workshops, or self-study.

Many physician leaders recognize the glaring gap in our training. We are more effective leaders through formal training and education. Over the last two decades, physicians have been obtaining MBAs, MHAs, MMMs, and a variety of other degrees and formal leadership certificates, including the CPE through the American Association for Physician Leadership and the FACHE through the American College of Healthcare Executives.

In 2019, for the first time, the number of employed physicians has exceeded those in private or solo practices. Many physicians, unfamiliar with corporate business structures and processes, are frustrated as their autonomy and practice environment have changed. I highly recommend graduate degrees, courses, and certificates for all physician leaders. The opportunity to network, share ideas, and learn the business side of medicine sets leaders up for success and the opportunity to discuss difficult scenarios and situations with other physician leaders.

DEFINING LEADERSHIP

How is effective leadership defined? I don't believe it is possible to truly define leadership with a single sentence or word, but we know good leadership when we see it or read about effective leaders within a historical context. From a purely corporate perspective, effective leadership leads to increased productivity, profitability, market share, or business growth. *Physician leaders are in the business of governing and managing others who provide a service within an organization.*

Good physician leadership includes these characteristics and behaviors:
- Strong ethics and high moral standards.
- Effective, timely communication.
- Outstanding self-organizational skills.
- Lifelong learning and development.
- Commitment to nurturing growth in others.
- Connections and positive inclusive relationships.
- Effective team building.

In healthcare, effective leadership leads to financially strong organizations with excellent patient safety records, growth, and capacity to adapt to change through agile, flexible responses to ongoing stresses — both external and internal.

There are many leadership styles; each one has advantages and disadvantages:

Democratic Leadership

Democratic leaders empower others and involve all stakeholders, including frontline staff, in many of the decision-making processes. They seek input and value individual opinion. A disadvantage of this style is the time necessary to seek input and analyze the qualitative and quantitative data.

Ultimately, the decision for an action plan is the responsibility of the leader but "paralysis by analysis" is a potential stumbling block. The time constraints put pressure on performance and potentially slow progress. Effective democratic leaders are able to switch gears and use different styles, depending on circumstances.

Autocratic Leadership

This is one of the least-effective leadership styles. These leaders often make unilateral decisions without seeking input from staff or colleagues. A path to disaster, this leadership style disempowers employees and can lead to high turnover, low morale, and decreased productivity. It is impossible to maintain a hegemonic culture using this style.

Laissez-Faire Leadership

This leadership style is exactly what the name implies: a "hands-off" style that empowers nearly every employee. A major advantage of this style is the degree of empowerment that allows for an individualistic style and input. However, without reasonable deadlines and frequent "check-ins" on progress, one team member can delay a project — and the leader is ultimately responsible. For this style to be effective, the leader must hold employees accountable.

Start-up companies often benefit from this approach, as it leads to rapid innovation, but as the company or organization matures, this style can be less effective as processes require standardization and uniformity in service or product delivery. In healthcare, this style is especially beneficial because physicians, for the most part, value their independence and autonomy.

Strategic Leadership

Strategic leaders sit at the interface between maintenance of operations and growth opportunities. This style is highly effective in healthcare as organizations seek to improve the quality of care while growing through service-line development. Strategic leaders seek opportunities and are keenly aware of internal and external circumstances that affect organizational performance. These leaders can incorporate characteristics from other leadership styles and quickly adapt to new situations. Those with charisma are often seen as visionary or future-oriented.

Transformational Leadership

Transformational leaders identify goals and tasks for employees and set expectations for organizational performance. Transformational leaders are change agents, seeking to improve existing processes through increased efficiency. A distinct advantage of this leadership style is pushing employees to go beyond their personal limits and learn new skills for a growth mindset. Employees who are not self-directed can be frustrated by this leadership style.

Transactional Leadership

Transactional leaders reward employees for their work. Traditionally, these leaders may offer performance bonuses for meeting production or safety goals, which is somewhat effective; however, a major disadvantage is that the "bonus" structure can encourage employees to do the minimum amount of work required to reach predetermined metrics.

Physician performance or quality bonus payments, for example, are commonly used "carrots" to encourage increased productivity. Once the physician has reached a metric, however, such as volume expectation, they may not have an incentive to work above and beyond this "floor of performance" unless they are rewarded.

Coach-Style Leadership

Daniel Goleman's book *Primal Leadership* suggests that a coaching style of leadership may best describe the qualities of the quiet leader. "The coaching style is the least-used tool in the leader's toolkit," Goleman says, "probably because it doesn't look like leadership."[1] Quiet leaders achieve breakthroughs by asking guided questions rather than giving orders or advice. What better way to empower your team?

Bureaucratic Leadership

In 1947, Max Weber first described the bureaucratic leadership style, in which an organization is highly regulated and controlled through a top-down approach, with the leader strictly enforcing rules and an established hierarchy. It is an ineffective way to lead a healthcare organization. By focusing on rules and regulations, these leaders lack the flexibility and agility to adapt to rapid changes, both internal and external.

Servant Leadership

Servant leadership is perhaps the oldest style of leadership, and it encompasses a broad range of positive attributes, attitudes, and behaviors. Literally, this leadership style means to serve others, which fosters and encourages growth in subordinates, creates a positive, inclusive team atmosphere, and contains a baked-in ethical philosophy of selflessness, honesty, and integrity. Servant leaders possess the following traits:

Strong decision-making skills. The servant leadership philosophy emphasizes people's needs. A good leader has to use their knowledge and experience to make a conscious choice in order to benefit the business or company, and it may not always be an easy choice. However, a strong servant leader isn't afraid to make an unpopular decision or offer critical feedback when necessary.

Emotional intelligence and self-awareness. A high degree of emotional intelligence gives servant leaders the capacity to take the perspectives and experiences of others into account in the decision-making process. They listen to understand. They understand the impact of their decisions — both good and bad.

Sense of Community. Building community is important for colleagues and coworkers, especially in a shared team environment. Creating a sense of community requires a foundation of cultural trust and a sense of belonging.

Foresight. Servant leaders use their past experiences to inform the expectations about the future. They think and plan ahead and predict the likely outcomes or consequences of potential actions. Servant leaders also know when to follow their instincts based on the knowledge they've gained over the years.

Ownership. Servant leaders take ownership and acknowledge errors or poor decisions.

Of the many leadership styles, the servant leadership style is best-suited for physicians, as it incorporates many of the attributes good physicians already possess: the capacity to listen and empathize with others.

Your leadership style will have an impact on your performance, others' perception of your leadership capabilities, and most importantly, your relationships. Effective leaders are capable of switching gears and using the best traits from each style, depending on the context or situation. Several tools are available to help you assess your leadership style, and I encourage you to use them. The AAPL has an online assessment tool you can complete; the results provide an analysis of your strengths and weaknesses. I also recommend hiring a leadership coach who can formally assess your style and recommend strategies and exercises to improve your weaknesses and maximize the potential of your strengths.

REFERENCE

1. Goleman D, Boyatzis R, and McKee A. *Primal Leadership: Unleashing the Power of Emotional Intelligence.* Boston: Harvard Business Review Press;2013.

CHAPTER 6

The Process of Investigating a Professional Behavior Complaint

Be curious, not judgmental.

– Walt Whitman

"I hear and I forget. I see and I remember.
I do and I understand."

– Chinese Proverb

INVESTIGATING PROFESSIONAL BEHAVIOR COMPLAINTS IS part of your leadership journey and experience. Creating a standardized process and approach helps you manage the situations and circumstances, which is important for several reasons.

First, your emotional response will decrease over time, and as you get more experience, your comfort with handling difficult situations will increase. More than a decade ago, as a newly minted chair of the department, I looked forward to the projects and progress, but I was wholly unprepared for investigating and navigating the professional conduct complaints. I believe that one *of the primary reasons many physicians do not aspire to a leadership role is the undesirable aspects of the leadership responsibility.*

Leadership positions transform your relationships with your peers. After I accepted the position as chair, I thought to myself, "How will I fulfill the duties assigned to this role without damaging professional or personal relationships?" It is a legitimate question, and navigating these waters is difficult.

It is easy to feel like Odysseus, in Homer's *Odyssey*, crossing the Strait of Messina between Scylla and Charybdis where he faced the decision to sail near Scylla, the monster, or Charybdis, the whirlpool. Sailing by Scylla meant the loss of a few lives as men were plucked off the deck. Sailing near the whirlpool meant the loss of the entire crew and ship. Either path led to destruction in some form. You, too, will make unpopular, uncomfortable decisions. The best decisions accomplish the goals with the least amount of professional, personal, and institutional disruption.

When you learn of a professional behavior complaint, your emotional response is likely a combination of anxiety, dread, and frustration. Acknowledge these emotions — they are a normal, natural result of receiving bad news. Then:

1. Take a deep breath. (This is about *their* behavior, not yours).
2. Avoid jumping to conclusions.
3. Seek the facts.

As a department chair, you have levels of support above you who have more experience and authority, such as a chief or president of the medical staff, vice president of the medical staff or affairs, or a chief medical officer. If these individuals are not available, seek guidance from a senior leader who has experience as a chair and can offer support. It is important to recognize that you are not alone; asking questions is more beneficial than making assumptions and mistakes. Always take the time to do it right.

BE CURIOUS

Behavior is a response to a series of events and circumstances, and we are all complex human beings with needs, motivations, and a personality. As much as we may want to know *why* someone engages in a behavior, the task is to strip away all emotion, all motives, and simply ask *who, what, when, where, and how?* Being curious means getting the whole story in chronological order starting with who was involved, what occurred, and if there are witnesses.

Behavior occurrence forms or anonymous reports are only one side of the story; they are not complete. A series of events usually occur prior to the behavior. (This is not always the case if there is an established pattern of behavior, and the event is one of many in a series of similar events with the same conduct involving the same physician.)

"Inheriting" a problem physician is not a pleasant experience. When I accepted a new position a few years ago, I was rightfully, and thankfully, alerted to ongoing concerns with a couple of providers. I was given background and context for any new behaviors. Having written reports and outcomes from prior professional behavior interventions is helpful as well.

Importantly, if the physician has an extensive history of professional behavior complaints, they do not get a "clean slate" with new leadership. Physicians are accountable for their actions at all times, and past transgressions matter. If you are in a leadership position and this is the fourth, fifth, or sixth complaint about the same physician, you are obligated to do everything possible to ensure the behavior stops.

In the past, high-earning physicians got a renewable "get out of jail free" card with no more than a slap on the wrist for each incident. Allowing a high-earning physician to continue to practice under a different set of rules is a double standard, and it erodes trust and staff morale.

Once the groundwork for the issue has been established, it is time to talk, preferably directly, with all parties involved.

TALK WITH PARTIES INVOLVED AND WITNESSES

For some passive-aggressive behaviors, there are no witnesses in the traditional sense. Chronic tardiness, incomplete charts, unanswered phone calls, texts, etc., do not require a witness, but they do require documentation or evidence. For most of the other professional conduct complaints, there are witnesses — always the attributed physician and any other individual or individuals involved in the behavior or incident.

Some institutions have anonymous reporting processes to protect the individual (victim or witness). Other institutions rely on frontline staff to report to managers or directors and provide formal written reports. If possible, speak directly with the parties involved and affirm you will protect their anonymity. Write down objective facts, times, exactly what was done or said, and by whom. If patient care was compromised as a result of the conduct, document that as well, as it may become a peer review concern.

In the past, I called or met with the attributed physician "over a cup of coffee" to discuss their first offense. It is a personal way to handle some professional behavior complaints, but I no longer engage in the cup of coffee conversations for several reasons.

First, there are potential legal ramifications, which I will discuss in more detail in the later chapters on legal matters. Second, there are no witnesses to your conversation. Third, if the attributed physician is of the opposite sex and you meet behind a closed door or a café for a discussion, you can be accused of sexual harassment. Fourth, if you do this for one physician, you must do it for all physicians to remain fair and objective. Lastly, which types of behaviors or individuals warrant a cup of coffee conversation? If fair, objective treatment can be questioned, it is not good practice. And as much as a casual conversation might seem beneficial, it is too informal and subjective.

I ensure I have a witness for one-on-one meetings with an attributed physician and take notes during the meeting, documenting who is present. This protects me and it protects the attributed physician.

Interviewing witnesses is a much simpler task than it might seem. If there is an opportunity, ask other staff and, if appropriate, patients what they saw or heard. If there is agreement and consistency among witnesses about what was heard or said, it is difficult for the attributed physician to provide a different story. In a professional conduct meeting, if there is agreement, I always state that several witnesses agree with the events as described. Witnesses and those affected by the physician's behavior must be protected from reciprocity or retaliation.

Some witnesses will not want to participate because "nothing is going to change anyway." One key to your success as a leader is to acknowledge how people feel. And in some cases, I have even told witnesses I am aware of long-standing concerns with an attributed physician. New leaders have an opportunity to set a new tone, but it takes some courage and grit. And sometimes it involves sticking your neck out and telling the witness that the situation can improve only if they are willing to speak out.

Lastly, it is important to caution the witnesses to not talk about the event with other parties. Their testimony is confidential, and it must remain confidential. This is necessary to maintain the integrity of the process and be respectful of everyone involved.

GATHER EVIDENCE

In addition to the initial documented reports and witness testimonials, physical evidence includes e-mails, texts, surveillance footage, badge access to entry/exit points, notes, pictures, social media posts, audio recordings, and video recordings. Evidence provides proof of conduct and is critical if the behavior is egregious and involves criminal charges.

Gather and store these documents in electronic or paper format. Do not personally keep the documents in your car, home, or any other location where they can be seen, lost, or stolen. Treat them as legal documents that must be kept as secure as possible. This not only protects you, it protects the confidentiality of the process. Evidence supports claims, and should the behavior lead to legal action by either party, it can mean the difference between successfully navigating the process to a positive outcome or the converse.

DISCUSS AND PLAN

Once the evidence is gathered, it is time to examine the bylaws and conduct code to plan the meeting with the attributed physician. If there is a professional behavior committee, inform the committee of the necessity of a meeting and schedule a pre-meeting to develop a plan on how to present the case to the attributed physician. The pre-meeting agenda includes asking for committee members' opinions on the issue and helps prevent being blindsided by unknown information or opinions. If there is no time for a formal pre-meeting, then meet 30 minutes before the start of the meeting with the physician to discuss the situation. It is not advisable to go in without prior discussion; making time for it will make the meeting far smoother for everyone.

Formal communication to the attributed physician about the meeting can be by a phone call (preferred method) or e-mail. A phone call is personal and less threatening than other forms of communication. For physicians who have a pattern of repeated behaviors, a certified letter is occasionally warranted. A certified letter communicates the seriousness of the meeting and event, and it symbolically escalates the need for change. In addition, if the process leads to legal action, it provides assurance the physician received notice.

Schedule the meeting, have a discussion with committee members or the CMO prior to the meeting, and communicate the time and place of the meeting to the attributed physician. The medical staff bylaws at your institution are your best guide, and it is imperative you follow the process outlined.

CONDUCT A PROFESSIONAL BEHAVIOR MEETING

No one ever looks forward to these meetings. Emotions run high; the attributed physician is anxious, angry, or both, and nearly everyone feels awkward discussing potentially embarrassing behaviors, events, or circumstances. Have copies of the signed (by the attributed physician) code of conduct, bylaws, and any reports with redacted names to preserve anonymity. If the physician is known to all parties, there is no need for formal introductions. If not, invite everyone to introduce themselves, then jump right in. It is not appropriate to start the meeting with small talk. Be polite, professional, sincere, and courteous. Remind everyone that the discussion is confidential and any matters discussed are not to be shared with anyone outside of the committee.

Thank the physician for taking time out of a busy day to attend the meeting. This is especially important for physicians who have never had a professional behavior issue that required a higher-level meeting. Give them a copy of their signed conduct form and state why the meeting is taking place.

At this point, pause and allow the attributed physician to tell their side of the story **without interruption.** The physician deserves the respect of some open airtime. Actively listen and take notes. Once the physician is finished, you can then ask questions or open the floor for further discussion.

On occasion, physicians will attempt to blame others for their own behavior. In high-stress situations, such as missing critical equipment needed for a difficult case, they may lose their composure, become angry, and engage in physically and verbally abusive behaviors. Let the physician vent but also tactfully remind them the reason for the meeting is their behavior; the missing equipment is a separate, important issue for another discussion.

An attributed physician's response in meetings can be categorized broadly into patterns of responses:

Acceptance: These physicians recognize the issue, apologize, accept responsibility, and state clearly that it will not happen again.

Hijacker: These physicians attempt to control the direction of the meeting, cast blame on others — even, on occasion, at the individual committee members if known to the attributed physician. Meetings can quickly spiral into a heated exchange with insults, foul language, and threats. In some cases, the behavior during the meeting is egregious enough to recommend termination or loss of privileges.

Quiet Acceptance: These physicians know and accept the behavior but are hesitant to provide the committee insight or promises to correct their behavior.

Wasting My Time: These physicians show up, state the meeting is a waste of time, and accept no responsibility.

Angry: These physicians are agitated and angry during the meeting.

I Am Here Again?: Repeat offenders are a problem and can be your greatest challenge.

Physicians who are first offenders and accept responsibility are usually no longer a problem; the meetings are smooth. Unfortunately, this is a rare instance. Most meetings involve a small group of physicians who have a pattern of repeated behaviors. Roughly 5% of the physicians create 95% of the problems or complaints.

DISPOSITION AND ACTION PLAN

Immediately after the meeting, ask the attributed physician to leave, and allow at least 15 to 30 minutes for an open discussion with other committee members. An open discussion permits members to confirm and validate the responses of the attributed physician. The goal is to agree on the disposition and an action plan. The document generated from the meeting is a legal document; the contents and accuracy protect the organization (see sample form in the Appendix). Below are sample letters sent to physicians after the meeting.

Sample Letters to a Physician

Sample Letter 1

Dr. J. Smith-Johnson   February 15, 2021
1234 Main Street USA

Dear Dr. Smith-Johnson:

Thank you for taking time out of your busy schedule to meet with the Professional Behavior Committee on Thursday, February 13, 2021. We appreciate the compassionate care you provide for the patients at St.

Anywhere, and we value your service and commitment. As discussed in the meeting, not returning pages in a timely fashion while on-call has led to delays in patient care in the ICU. Additionally, numerous nurses have also reported a rude and condescending tone when they ask questions or request clarification.

As you revealed in the meeting, you have had a difficult year in your personal life that has impacted your attitude at work. We appreciate your honesty and respect your privacy, and as stated in the meeting, the discussion is confidential. Several of us recommended counseling or a temporary reduction in your workload to help offset current stressors affecting your work. You have a long-standing history of providing excellent, timely care, and we are here to support you.

The committee requests that you meet with me and the Chief Medical Officer, Dr. Jones, in approximately one month for a follow-up discussion. If you have any questions or concerns or need to meet with Dr. Jones or me prior to the next meeting, please do not hesitate to contact either of us.

Respectfully,

Matthew Mazurek, MD, MHA, CPE, FASA
Chair, Professional Behavior Committee

Sample Letter 2

Dr. Miller-Smith   August 4, 2021
1234 Main Street USA

Dear Dr. Miller-Smith:

Thank you for taking time out of your busy schedule to meet with the Professional Behavior Committee on August 1, 2021. As discussed in the meeting, this is the third time in less than four months staff has witnessed you using inappropriate and foul language angrily directed toward staff in the operating room. The latest incident also included you throwing an instrument across the room. As physicians, we have a responsibility to model professional behavior and treat all colleagues, staff, and patients with respect.

We understand your frustration that instruments you frequently use were not contained in the setup trays, which prompted you to berate the staff. We also agree the lack of preparedness for surgery through missing instruments is a patient safety concern. However, an inappropriate response creates an unsafe working environment. Per our discussion, this Committee is drafting a letter of concern to the OR Director, Pamela Hart, and the Chief Medical Officer, Dr. Fine, regarding the continued problem of missing instruments.

The Committee recommends you attend a formal professional behavior management program. We realize attendance at this program will inconvenience you and interrupt patient care, and we desire to minimize the impact this has on your practice. Failure to complete or participate in the program may lead to termination of privileges.

You have a longstanding reputation of providing excellent care for your patients at St. Anywhere, and your patients clearly seek the care you provide, and your colleagues respect your opinions and care. However, as physicians, we have a responsibility to maintain a respectful, collegial, and safe work environment. If possible, schedule a meeting with me within one week to discuss options for enrolling in a program and altering your schedule.

Respectfully,

Matthew Mazurek, MD, MHA, CPE, FASA
Chief of Staff, St. Anywhere

CHAPTER 7

Case Examples

*"No man is your enemy, no man is your
friend, every man is your teacher."*

– FLORENCE SCOVEL SHINN

*"Men at some time are masters of their fates:
The fault, dear Brutus, is not in our stars,
But in ourselves, that we are underlings."*

– CASSIUS TO BRUTUS, JULIUS CAESAR

MOST OF THE CASE EXAMPLES presented here are based on my experiences during the past 10 years in a variety of leadership roles. I also include cases from other physician leaders who have shared their experiences. Lastly, some of the higher-profile cases that have made national headlines are presented as examples of egregious, often criminal, behavior. Names and exact circumstances have been altered to preserve anonymity. The case studies are presented in a narrative, dialogue format to illustrate the human side and soft skills required to successfully navigate and resolve professional behavior issues.

Finally, the quotes I use to introduce this section are salient as I describe my own emotional response in these cases as I tell these stories. Every case was a learning experience. Following each case presentation, I briefly discuss the disposition and letters or actions addressed to the physician. I hope you find them useful.

SEXUAL HARASSMENT BEHAVIOR

This section may be difficult for some readers, as some stories are "triggering." These examples describe inappropriate conduct and what may be incorrectly construed as "minor" offenses. In my opinion, any behavior that falls under the definition of "sexual harassment" is a serious matter.

The cases I am presenting involve men accused of harassing women because these are the cases I am familiar with; however, it is important to note that women can harass men, too. Additionally, same-sex harassment occurs.

Some men may feel insecure reporting harassment, and some women and men may hesitate to report harassment from someone of the same sex due, again, to stigma or fear of being judged unfairly.[1] I urge you to cast aside the "traditional" stereotypes and investigate the incident purely based on the behavior itself.

Case 1: A Love Letter

I had just been called to the OR director's office. It was a late Thursday afternoon, and I was tired after doing several vascular cases. Jackie, the OR director, handed me a small, folded note with dog-eared edges. It looked exactly like the notes we passed in physics class in high school. As she handed me the note, Jackie said, "I was just given this note by the instructor for our scrub tech students." I opened the note and began reading, silently, in Spanish:

Espero que no lo tome a mal. Pero cuando miro profundamente en las piscinas de tus ojos azules, me encuentro perdido. Quizas podamos tomar una taza de café si tienes la oportunidad.

(Translation: I hope you do not take this the wrong way. But when I look deep into the pools of your blue eyes, I find myself lost. Maybe we can have a cup of coffee if you get the chance.)

"Who wrote *this*?" I asked and handed back the note, a bit dumbfounded.

Jackie quickly replied, "It was Dr. Z. I am not surprised, and I am certain you are not either. I think you know the student, as she has been in the OR for the past couple of weeks. She is terribly upset and simply did not know what to do. She is afraid of stirring up trouble, so she spoke with her instructor at the technical school."

I was disgusted and I was fuming angry. I thought to myself, "What if this was my daughter?" As my emotional response faded, I felt that awkward sense of dread about what had to be done. It was going to be ugly, embarrassing, and awkward for everyone. But my first concern was for the student.

Jackie assured me the student would not be assigned to Dr. Z's room again. I asked whether the student felt safe and comfortable continuing her rotation. She did, and I told Jackie to tell the instructor and student that we were going to address the concerns.

This was a case that could not and should not be handled with a "collegial discussion" and a warning. This case, following due process, warranted a meeting with the Professional Behavior Committee, of which I was chair. There was no doubt this letter was blatant sexual harassment, and if handled improperly, could quickly escalate into an embarrassing story in the newspaper and a lawsuit. Furthermore, there could be other behaviors similar to this that have not been reported.

I immediately sent an e-mail to the Professional Behavior Committee members asking for availability for a meeting within the next week. I now had to confront the attributed physician and request he attend a meeting with the committee. These phone conversations are always difficult — I had known this surgeon professionally for years, and we were on a first-name basis.

I dialed his number, thinking about how to open the dialogue. As he picked up and said "Hello," I replied, "Hey Jim, sorry to bother you. I know you are busy, but I need to ask you a couple of questions, and this may seem awkward. A couple of days ago I was made aware of a note you wrote to a student. Did you write this note?"

After what seemed like an infinite pause, he sheepishly said, "Yes."

"Jim, I need you to meet with me and the Professional Behavior Committee next Monday afternoon at 5 p.m.," I replied. "I know you are pressed for time, and you have clinic until 4 p.m. that day. Can you meet with us at this time?" "Yeah, I can meet," he replied. Before I hung up, I affirmed, "OK, thank you Jim, we will see you on Monday."

This case example is not a "he said, she said." There was physical evidence: a note. What occurred was obvious, and what needed to be done was obvious.

The attributed physician felt awkward and embarrassed. At the same time, it was awkward to have these conversations without making it worse. In my phone call, I was direct and to the point. I did not socialize with this physician outside work, but I knew his personality, and he was not one for having casual conversations in the OR. He was relatively quiet, went about his business, and mainly kept to himself. Rather than stumble my way through a phone conversation with some small talk, I was professional, courteous, and direct.

Imagine, however, if the conversation had gone differently. He answers the call, and I say, "Hey Jim, how are you today?" He replies, "I'm OK. What do you want?"

I begin, "Well, I was handed this note that you wrote to a stud---."

He cuts me off, "That little note? How the f**k did you get that note? That was not a note for you or anyone else. It is a private matter. You know, this hospital has been screwing with me for years, and I am sick of this s**t! And now you have the guts to call me about a stupid little note I sent to a student! It is harmless. I give a little compliment and want to know if she wants to have some coffee? It is not like I am asking her out for a date or dinner. What is wrong with you guys — always making a mountain out of a mole hill!! You know, Matt, I used to like working with you, but now that you are on 'the other side,' I am not sure I want to work with you anymore."

Shaken and shocked, how do I reply? What do I say now? The meeting must happen. Obviously, this is not how events transpired, but ask yourself how you would respond in this situation.

As difficult as it might be, take a deep breath. That last bit of conversation was personal — even biting. Here is a surgeon I have gotten along well with for years in the OR who no longer wants to work with me because now I am a "cop" for the hospital, working against, not for, the physicians.

It is imperative to compartmentalize and contain your emotions, cast aside the personal jab, and move forward with what is now a painful and difficult conversation.

In his response, he minimizes the note and mentions his perceptions about how much the hospital has been "screwing with him for years." Deflection and blame are powerful tactics attributed physicians use to minimize and sometimes justify their own behavior.

Jim has hijacked the conversation. Acknowledge his emotional response. Do not respond with your own emotional response. Acknowledge his anger. Validate how he feels. It has nothing to do with the note or the behavior, and it has everything to do with being keenly aware that you are now in a situation that can escalate or cool down. The only way you can remain calm is to check your own temperature.

I state, "Jim, I know you are pretty upset. I get that, but I need you to attend a professional behavior meeting on Monday to discuss this letter."

He responds, "And if I don't show up, then what?"

Obviously, the meeting is going to occur at some point, and the sooner, the better. I reply, "Jim, the quicker this gets resolved, the better. I know you don't feel this note is a big deal, but we need to meet to have a discussion."

He says, "You guys are wasting your time and my time, but I will be there."

The afternoon of the meeting, the four other members of the Professional Behavior Committee meet with me in a small conference room overlooking the Tucson skyline. The meeting was scheduled for 4 p.m. We wait. When 4:30 comes and goes, we all wonder if we are wasting our precious time.

I say, "He might not show up, and if he doesn't, none of you are obligated to stay past 5 p.m." Finally, he shows up at 4:45 p.m. in a huff and obviously not wanting to be at the meeting.

Without apology, he plops down in a chair. I tell him why we are here and hand him a copy of the professional conduct policy that he had signed when his privileges were renewed. I remind him that our discussion is confidential, and we respect his privacy and appreciate his service here at the hospital. After a moment, I give him a copy of the letter he had given the student and ask if he had written and given the note. He says he did.

Prior to his arrival, the committee had discussed key points of discussion regarding this event. In accordance, I first explain to Dr. Z that this conduct constitutes sexual harassment. Second, I communicate that the power dynamic involves domains of age, status, and gender. A middle-aged male physician should not be approaching a student verbally or through correspondence of any kind at work. The issue is cut and dry. I then explain that the committee will discuss disposition, and he can expect a letter delineating any further action required by the committee.

After his departure, we all agreed the matter was egregious enough to formally request he complete a course on sexual harassment at his expense. The message needed to be clear that the behavior will not be tolerated. Additionally, our actions and response reflect the organization and the medical staff is serious about addressing these concerns.

Letter to the Attributed Physician

Dear Dr. Z:

Thank you for taking the time to meet with the Professional Behavior Committee on April 5. The committee would first like to say that you have a long history of providing great care at Alpha Health; however, as physicians, we have a responsibility to respect boundaries between our patients, trainees, and students. While you may feel the note to the student was somewhat trivial, the student did not interpret the note in this manner. The note and its message are a form of sexual harassment, and per the Code of Conduct, there is zero tolerance for this behavior.

The committee, therefore, recommends, at your expense and convenience, you take an online or in-person course on sexual harassment. We will provide you with a list of available courses, or you can choose an alternate course that must be approved by this committee. You have 60 calendar days from receipt of this letter to provide proof of completion of the course.

If you fail to complete the course within 60 calendar days, the committee may, at its discretion, recommend summary suspension of privileges. It is not our intent for you to lose the privilege to practice at Alpha Health. We thank you for your time. If you have any questions or concerns, please do not hesitate to ask me or one of the other committee members.

Respectfully,

Matt Mazurek, MD, MHA, CPE, FASA
Chair, Professional Behavior Committee

Case 2: The Off-Handed Comment

Late one winter night, one of my colleagues was called in to do a complex case on a critically ill patient who required postoperative ventilation and admission to the ICU. Most of us who do acute care in the hospital have been in similar situations. We are tired, stressed, and in a high-pressure environment. The time is conducive to someone saying or doing something inappropriate.

And this was the case at 2 a.m. as my colleague dropped off his patient in the ICU. As the anesthesiologist gave report and a "hand-off" to the nurse, the nurse casually mentioned everything was OK, and he could go home. According to her, he said in a grumbling tone, "Might as well stay here. I am not getting any at home anyway!"

Is this sexual harassment? Everyone can agree that it's inappropriate, but some might argue that it's not sexual harassment. I disagree. First, the comment was unsolicited. Second, the power and gender dynamic and nature of what was said was sexual even though it was not about the nurse. Was the nurse uncomfortable with the comment? Yes, she was, and she filed a report.

As I read the summary of circumstances and the report, I noted there were no witnesses who could confirm what was stated. I faced the classic dilemma of "he said, she said." Fortunately, this was the first professional conduct complaint about this physician, so there was no established pattern of behavior. Still, I was concerned about the physician's personal circumstances that would lead him to make such a statement. Obviously, his personal life was not in order. Was this a red flag for other issues?

Rather than convene a formal meeting, I decided it was best to ask my colleague about the situation that night and whether he recalled having said what was stated. I called him one afternoon, "Brad, how are you?"

He sounded surprised and said tentatively, "I'm OK, what's up?"

"Well, Brad," I replied, "I wish I were calling you for a different reason, but unfortunately, I have to ask you an awkward question. Do you recall last week when you were on-call and dropped off a patient in the ICU about 2 a.m.?"

"Yes."

"Well, there was a complaint about something you said soon after you gave report. Specifically, you mentioned something about not being happy about going home. This is awkward for me to say this, but the nurse said you told her you 'weren't getting any at home.' I know this is somewhat embarrassing for me to tell you this, but I need to know whether or not you said that."

In a lower, serious tone, he said, "Really? I guess I did, but I did not think it was a big deal. She didn't say anything to me."

I replied, "Regardless of how you may feel about this, the nurse thought it was inappropriate enough to report, and it made her uncomfortable. I know this is the first time you have had a professional behavior complaint attributed to you, and I know you realize this cannot happen again. I will have to type up a formal letter regarding the points of our discussion and have you sign it."

"Ok," he said, and that was the first and last event.

Afterward, I approached the nurse and the nurse manager in the ICU. I apologized and reassured the nurse it would not happen again. Staff, students, or colleagues who report this behavior need to feel protected. The fear of reciprocity and retaliation is real, and this does lead to under-reporting events.

Letter to the Attributed Physician

Dear Dr. H:

Thank you for taking the time to speak with me the other day regarding the events that occurred in the ICU on February 8, 2021. As you know, making inappropriate comments about your personal life in front of a nurse may be misinterpreted. You acknowledged you stated what was reported, and I appreciate your honesty.

I know you realize this type of comment is serious, and if another incident occurs, you will be referred to the Professional Behavior Committee. Please sign this copy of the letter acknowledging our conversation and the contents of this letter. You have a long history of providing excellent care, and we appreciate your hard work. Please do not hesitate to contact me if you have any further questions.

Kind regards,

Matt Mazurek, MD, MHA, CPE, FASA
Chair, Department of Anesthesia
Alpha Health

Case 3: Working After Hours

Dr. W is a second-year female radiology resident. Her program director, Dr. S, is a nationally recognized radiologist who has many valuable national connections. He is a married father of two young children whose photos he proudly displays in his office. He invites Dr. W to meet with him at dinner at an upscale Italian restaurant to discuss her career aspirations and a potential research project of national importance in the field.

The evening is social, and there is no discussion of research. While helping Dr. W put on her coat, Dr. S's hand lingers on her lower back, which Dr. W finds uncomfortable but ultimately dismisses. In the following weeks,

Dr. S calls and texts Dr. W several times on her cell phone, telling her that he "thoroughly enjoyed the dinner" and would like to meet with her again to "discuss her career."

Dr. W asks Dr. S to stop contacting her on her cell phone. He texts her back and notes that "it is going to be hard for him or the rest of his division to work with her in the future" if she is not willing to spend the time meeting after hours to work on research. He states that he finds "her vivacious personality difficult to get out of his head" and is "disappointed" that she is not interested in spending time outside of work to pursue their "shared academic interests."

He persists in sending her e-mail, some with direct links to scientific articles he has written. Dr. W is uncertain how to proceed, and she searches for general information on sexual misconduct and harassment in medicine.

Based on her research, Dr. W determines that she has experienced sexual harassment. She reports this to her institutional GME office and department chair. After an internal investigation, Dr. S is removed as the program director and ultimately resigns from his position to pursue a job in a teleradiology practice.

This case is one of thousands that have occurred throughout the years. In a 1995 large cross-sectional survey, roughly 50% of faculty women reported sexual harassment compared with only 5% of men.[2] The power dynamic in the relationships in academic medicine can be a barrier to reporting sexual harassment, as the field of medicine has traditionally been dominated by men. Women who report sexual harassment face the same barriers now that they always have. Specifically, will the claim be supported and believed? Will there be retribution? What will happen to my career advancement if I am perceived as a whistleblower or complainer? Will nothing happen? *There is a lot of personal risk in reporting sexual harassment.*

TITLE VII

Title VII of the Civil Rights Act of 1964 generally prohibits discrimination in the workplace but does not contain an express prohibition against harassment. The Supreme Court, however, has interpreted the statute to prohibit certain forms of harassment, including sexual harassment. Since first recognizing the viability of a Title VII harassment claim in a unanimous

1986 decision, the Supreme Court has also established legal standards for determining when offensive conduct amounts to a Title VII violation and when employers may be held liable for such actionable harassment.[3]

The Equal Employment Opportunity Commission (EEOC) is responsible for filing claims of sexual harassment. For clarity, I am providing an excerpt from the EEOC website regarding the nature of sexual harassment:

> It is unlawful to harass a person (an applicant or employee) because of that person's sex. Harassment can include "sexual harassment" or unwelcome sexual advances, requests for sexual favors, and other verbal or physical harassment of a sexual nature.
>
> Harassment does not have to be of a sexual nature, however, and can include offensive remarks about a person's sex. For example, it is illegal to harass a woman by making offensive comments about women in general.
>
> Both victim and the harasser can be either a woman or a man, and the victim and harasser can be the same sex. Although the law doesn't prohibit simple teasing, offhand comments, or isolated incidents that are not very serious, harassment is illegal when it is so frequent or severe that it creates a hostile or offensive work environment or when it results in an adverse employment decision (such as the victim being fired or demoted). The harasser can be the victim's supervisor, a supervisor in another area, a co-worker, or someone who is not an employee of the employer, such as a client or customer.[4]

The #MeToo Movement and One Medical System's Response

The #MeToo movement has prompted organizations and businesses to proactively address and eradicate the pervasive problem of sexual harassment in the workplace. Interestingly, in 2017, the Mayo Clinic updated its policies on sexual harassment and developed an institutional approach to the problem. To my knowledge, this is the first healthcare organization to implement such a targeted initiative with such broad and sweeping scope. The process the Mayo Clinic used, outlined below, illustrates the complexity, sensitivity, and difficulty in managing sexual harassment claims[5]:

1. The allegation is assigned to a trained Human Resources investigator.
2. If there is an immediate danger to the reporter or others, the employee

whose conduct is under investigation (the accused) may be placed on administrative leave. The reporter is provided support by Human Resources advisors and offered Employee Assistance Program services. The accused is also offered these services.

3. An experienced Human Resources investigator and partner interview the reporter, the accused, and any potential witnesses. Relevant information is gathered, including, if authorized, an investigation of electronic communications between relevant parties. The accused has the opportunity to respond to allegations and present his or her version of events, along with any relevant evidence or potential witnesses.

4. An investigative report is prepared and presented to departmental leadership, Human Resources, the Personnel Committee, and the Legal Department. A decision is made based on review of all evidence, interviews, and the investigative report and taking mitigating factors into account. Principles of a Fair and Just Culture are used as a guide for consistency. The severity of the alleged infraction, prior history, and any past or current corrective actions are all considered.

5. If the allegations are deemed to be substantiated, appropriate action is taken. The action taken will depend on the seriousness of the infraction(s) and could include coaching, written warning, a final written warning with or without suspension, or termination of employment.

6. If termination proceedings are recommended, the accused is notified of the intent to terminate. Resignation in lieu of termination may be requested and is at the discretion of Mayo Clinic to allow in limited situations.

7. For the physician and scientist staff, a separate and independent 3-person panel of peers reviews the evidence, including the recommendation for termination, and makes the final decision. The panel has the authority to reinterview anyone if deemed necessary.

8. If terminated, the employee may choose to appeal pursuant to the Mayo Corrective Action policy. If appealed, a second independent 3-person panel of peers reviews all evidence and is empowered to uphold or overturn the corrective action decision. The panel is also empowered to reinterview.

9. If state law requires that the conduct giving rise to termination be reported to a state licensing board, an appropriate report is filed.

10. Post-action activities include providing closing communication to the complainant (including instructions to report any retaliation), debriefing senior leadership, and responding to external requests for references. The situation is analyzed, and opportunities for improvement, if any, are identified.

INAPPROPRIATE AND ABUSIVE PHYSICIAN-PATIENT RELATIONSHIPS

Physicians have ended their careers through inappropriate relationships or abuse of the patient-doctor relationship. The power dynamic between the physician and patient creates a situation where mutual consent is not possible. This is why it is imperative for physicians to maintain boundaries with their patients.

Dr. Larry Nassar, former USA Gymnastics team doctor, who sexually abused hundreds of female athletes and pleaded guilty to federal child pornography charges, was sentenced to 60 years in prison on December 7, 2017. On November 22, 2017, he pleaded guilty in state court to seven charges of first-degree sexual assault and entered another guilty plea a week later to three additional charges of sexual assault. On January 24, 2018, he was sentenced to an additional 40 to 175 years in prison, set to begin after Nassar serves the 60-year federal prison sentence for child pornography.

Another recent case involves a physician who arranged a plea agreement after being charged with four felonies for alleged sexual misconduct with two patients. In summary, one patient claimed she was raped in his office on multiple occasions and, furthermore, he wrote opioid prescriptions for the patient. In a prior incident, the physician had a relationship with another patient that was, according to accounts, mutual and ended without incident.[6]

To protect yourself and the organization from an unfounded claim of inappropriate physical exams, touching, or questions, it is best practice to consider the Garman Guidelines[7]:

1. Allow patients to disrobe and dress in private and offer cover gowns and appropriate drapes. (Yes, some physicians do not practice these simple steps.)

2. Have one of your office staff in the room whenever possible, especially during breast and pelvic exams. (I have talked to many physicians who feel this is silly and an added burden on their office staff. However, many women are very offended if these exams are done without another person in attendance. It would be reasonable to have your office nurse ask your patient if she would prefer to have an attendant in the room.)

3. Improve your communication with the patient about the reasons for and methods of examinations. (If you feel a breast examination for axillary lymphadenopathy is necessary for a hand infection, tell the patient why you are doing it.)

4. Avoid any flirtatious behavior toward patients. (Since you are perceived as a "power" figure, the patient may be hesitant to complain directly to you about jokes or other "innocent" behavior.)

5. Ask someone else to review your office procedures regarding physical exams with a view toward avoiding any risky procedures or making necessary changes. (One series of complaints was dealt with by asking the physician's female office staff to review and change standard examination procedures to avoid future problems.)

John R. Sealy, MD, an expert on the subject of sexual addiction and sexual misconduct by physicians, has provided training to investigators. He provided this valuable missive, entitled "General Truths" to identify known dynamics of sexual misconduct involving physicians:

1. No matter how difficult or boundary testing the patient/client may be, IT IS ALWAYS the professional's responsibility to maintain appropriate boundaries or, if unable to do so, to refer the patient/client for competent help or counsel.

2. Sexual misconduct usually begins with relatively minor boundary violations. Boundaries include time, place/space, money, gift/services, clothing, and language.

3. Crossing boundaries by a professional is almost always a power differential.

4. The professional must refrain from obtaining personal gratification at the expense of the patient/client. The main source of personal pleasure comes from the professional pleasure gained in helping the

patient/client. The fee for professional services is the only material satisfaction a physician should receive directly from the patient/client.

5. No level of training, nor school of medicine, school of law, school of dentistry, or school of psychotherapy confers immunity from sexual misconduct by a professional.

Other "red flags" that push the boundaries of professionalism include:

- You start talking to the patient about the patient's personal life.
- You check your personal appearance before a particular patient arrives.
- A patient is scheduled at the end of the day to "allow for more time."
- You allow your staff to go home early while you interact with a particular patient.
- You offer the patient food or drink.
- You exchange gifts or hugs with a patient.
- You offer free care to a particular patient.
- You call the patient at home when the condition does not warrant it.
- You meet the patient outside the office.

An unfortunate circumstance occurs when the script is flipped, and the patient flirts with or tries to seduce the physician. It is common for male patients to make inappropriate comments to attractive female physicians; as well, female patients can and do try to seduce male physicians.[7] When a patient makes an inappropriate comment or flirts, establishing clear boundaries is a priority. To avoid any accusations of impropriety, leave the exam room and find a staff member to witness the remainder of the visit. Another strategy is deflection. Don't acknowledge the statement and move onto clinical subject matter.[8]

Interestingly, psychiatrists are more likely to be disciplined for sexual boundary violations than their peers. Several factors could increase psychiatrists' risk of sexual boundary violations. They often work in isolation, out of view of other professionals. They have more personal contact and longer and more sessions with individual patients, hence more opportunity to become intimate with them.[9] Maintaining boundaries and encouraging physicians to ensure following respectful processes with dignity and respect diminishes the opportunities for sexual misconduct or inappropriate relationships.

PASSIVE-AGGRESSIVE BEHAVIOR

Case 1: I'm Late. So What?

It was 6:56 on a Wednesday morning, and Dr. S was nowhere to be found. Over several months, Dr. S had arrived later and later until finally, her behavior was affecting on-time starts in the OR. The impact was broad: trickle-down delays bottlenecked the rest of the schedule, leading to increased patient wait times, lost opportunity costs, dissatisfied surgeons, and increased labor costs.

A person can be chronically late for myriad reasons, but when it continues unabated, it's a problem. My first course of action, as department chair, was to ask why she could not show up on time.

Late on a Thursday afternoon, I summoned Dr. S to my office. "Dr. S," I said, "I am concerned about your arrival time in the morning, especially when you are on-call. All of us know we must complete pre-ops by 7:20 a.m. at the latest for our 7:30 a.m. start time. Is there any particular reason why you are arriving late?"

Dr. S replied, "You know I have a unique situation at home, and it has been difficult. I am a single parent with no help."

"Yes," I said, "you have made me aware of this in the past, but lately, you are arriving later and later, and the ORs are delayed. We have an obligation to arrive on time and prepare our patients. The surgeons have approached me about this as well."

She sulked a little bit, then quickly turned away, threw her hands up in the air, and blurted, "I will try!"

The change was short-lived. For the next two weeks, she arrived on time. Then, gradually, she arrived later and later until, two months later, the old pattern of chronic tardiness had returned. Unfortunately, the next-level intervention required a formal meeting with Dr. S to talk about the seriousness of the problem and discuss and document a performance improvement plan.

In the corporate world, performance improvement plans (PIP) are often mocked as "The First Step Toward Firing You Plan." The goal of a PIP is to set, measure, and document performance. In this case, arrival times are documented daily, as all physicians "punch in" via a time clock.

The PIP was just part of the meeting; we also discussed our willingness to assist Dr. S in getting help at home. We remained sensitive and empathetic to her situation, but we emphasized that we could not allow the behavior to continue. Everyone is expected to arrive on time. Ignoring the problem erodes morale, establishes a double standard for performance, and can create and perpetuate a negative cultural atmosphere. Fortunately, Dr. S started to arrive on time consistently, and her behavior changed.

"Has anyone seen Dr. M?" I ask. The charge nurse in pre-op replies, "Dr. Mazurek, you know as well as I do, he will be here when he gets here. All of us are tired of it, but it's been going on for years, and he won't change."

Dr. M is a surgeon who, for *years,* arrived late and apathetic. I knew from my interactions with him that he knew he should arrive on time, and in fact, he hinted that he *could* arrive on time, but he adamantly refused. For some physicians, this type of passive-aggressive behavior is only meant to make a statement: *I can do what I want and when I want.* It is an exercise in demonstrating control and power.

As Chair of Anesthesia, my only recourse for a few years was bringing this behavior to the attention of the Chair of Surgery. Despite these efforts, nothing changed. When I became Chief of Staff, Elect, one of my responsibilities was Chair of Professional Behavior. I now had the leverage I needed to address the issue. I made a business case to colleagues and hospital leadership. An idle OR is an expensive resource to waste. The exact dollar-per-minute cost of OR time is difficult to calculate, but the lost labor and opportunity cost is enormous over the course of a year. Additionally, if other surgeons who want OR block time are waiting in line, it does not make sense to allow a surgeon to consistently arrive late — often egregiously late.

As I had known Dr. M for many years, I asked the OR director if we should set up a meeting with him to discuss the issue. She agreed. We set up the meeting for the following week after I spoke with Dr. M.

Despite this behavior, Dr. M was an approachable, agreeable person who could be sarcastic at times, but the sarcasm was rarely directed at an individual.

I picked up the phone and began with "Joe, it's Matt. Jane and I would like to talk with you about one in the afternoon next week about the OR schedule. Are you free on Wednesday at 3 p.m.?"

Joe replied, "That's at the end of my block that day, so depending on how the OR goes, sure."

The following Wednesday, Dr. M arrived late for surgery, started late, and went 30 minutes over his scheduled block time. It was now 3:30 p.m. and Jane and I patiently waited in her office. Both of us knew this would happen, which is one of the reasons we scheduled the meeting at the end of the day.

A few minutes later, Dr. M arrived and said in a somewhat jovial tone, "Hey, what's going on?"

"Joe, have a seat," I replied. "We want to discuss block times with you, but first, Jane and I are concerned with your arrival time for your 7:30 start. Most of the time you arrive at 8:00 a.m., and the OR does not get started until 8:15 a.m. Patients are complaining and staff are complaining about having to stay after 3 p.m. when they work in your room. It is a big problem, and we appreciate what you do for the patients here, but you need to arrive by 7:15 a.m. to start the day."

Without pause, he replied, "Yeah, I know, I can't seem to get things together in the morning. I can push my start time to 8 a.m. if it's no big deal."

Letter to the Attributed Physician

Dear Dr. M:

Thank you for taking the time to meet with Jane Jones, the OR director, and me on August 5, 2021. We recognize and appreciate the excellent care you provide for the patients at St. Anywhere. As discussed at the meeting, chronic tardiness impacts patient satisfaction and OR efficiency, and increases costs for providing surgical services. Last month, 120 hours of overtime was paid out due to late starts. As discussed, you suggested a start time of 8 a.m. Unfortunately, we cannot accommodate this request, as staff are scheduled for 8-hour shifts, and all other surgical service lines start at 7:30 a.m.

If there is anything we can do to assist you in arriving by 7:15 a.m., please let us know. Per our OR policy addressing on-time starts, all physicians are expected to be present and available to start the OR day at 7:15 a.m.. Of course, extenuating circumstances are allowed, but per policy, no more than three late arrivals are allowed per quarter. If more than three late arrivals are accrued in any given quarter, per policy, *you may lose your block start time.* We do not desire for you to lose your block time, but it is a professional expectation to respect your patients' and colleagues' time.

Thank you again for meeting with us. If you have questions, don't hesitate to ask either Jane Jones or me how we can assist you or clarify any concerns.

Kind regards,

Matthew Mazurek, MD
Chair, Department of Anesthesia
St. Anywhere Hospital

Case 2: Bad Jokes at a Bad Time — All the Time

"Hey Matt! What do you call a _____ who has _____?" John blurts out at the start of a case. I reply, "John, I dunno, what?" He says, "A _____." You can fill in the blanks. On occasion, this particular surgeon took particular delight in telling racist and off-color jokes. Needless to say, a majority of the OR staff just rolled along with it because it was "Dr. M," and that was just part of his schtick in the OR. His jokes were only about his particular ethnicity, and he believed he was somehow "entitled" to make fun of his own culture, but it got old. I was tired of it, and so were a lot of staff members, but nothing really ever changed despite our requests that he stop.

Nursing, radiology, and medical students often rotated through the OR, and finally, one morning, Dr. M told yet another racist joke. At the end of the day, the student notified her preceptor, and the next day I was asked to speak with our OR director about the formal complaint from the student. As I was not present, I did not hear the joke, but that is immaterial. Two other witnesses to the joke attested to the nature and confirmed that it was a racist joke.

I had a long-standing, positive working relationship with this physician, and I was relatively new in my role as Chair of the Professional Behavior Committee. I decided to have the one-on-one conversation. I did not know if it would work given his history of telling these types of jokes for many years. I asked Dr. M if he could have a talk with me the following day after he completed his cases. He agreed.

We met in my office, and I got right to the point.

"John," I said, "you have been telling racist and sexist jokes for years, and I know you think it is no big deal, but it is. A student heard one of your jokes a couple of days ago and reported it. If this continues, you could lose your privileges. We have a responsibility to behave in a manner consistent with our status as physicians. You know this."

John replied, "Yeah, Matt, I get it. I will pipe down a bit. People sure are sensitive and literally cannot take a joke anymore."

"Thanks John." I said. "I do have to type up a letter and have you sign it with the points of our brief conversation."

This case was particularly simple, and the fact I had gained Dr. M's respect and trust over several years made the conversation easy. New leaders who step into this situation do not have the luxury of time to build relationships and trust, and a cup of coffee conversation may or may not go well. Dr. M stopped telling these types of jokes, and the problem was solved.

Letter to the Attributed Physician

Dear Dr. M:

Thank you for taking the time to speak with me about your behavior in the OR and telling inappropriate jokes. You have a long track record of taking excellent care of the patients at St. Anywhere, but this behavior detracts from our mission to provide a safe environment to care for patients and offer rotations for students from many different programs. The students and staff deserve to learn and work in a respectful environment.

You have acknowledged your jokes may be offensive and have stated you will stop telling inappropriate jokes in the OR or any other location in the hospital. Please sign and acknowledge that you agree with the statements in this letter. If there is a lapse and another inappropriate joke is shared with staff or students, you will need to attend a meeting with the Professional Behavior Committee for further disposition. Again, thank you for your commitment to St. Anywhere. If you have any further questions or concerns, please do not hesitate to contact me.

Warm regards,

Matthew Mazurek, MD, MHA, CPE, FASA
Chair, Professional Behavior Committee
Chief of Staff

Case 3. I Hate My Job and St. Anywhere Sucks

"Nothing ever changes around here! It sucks!" Dr. Z yelled. "I put the order in for the antibiotics one hour ago, and the patient is septic. Does *anyone* seem to care? Where is the charge nurse?"

Dr. Z was notorious for complaining about everything wrong with the hospital — from the parking lot lights to the computers and paging system. Most of us have experienced or know physicians who never seem to be happy with their job or the hospital or clinic.

The nurse replied, "Dr. Z, we are short-staffed, and the charge nurse is at a code in the ICU."

Dr. Z was, quick to reply, fist clinched, "We are short-staffed? That seems to be the buzzword of the day up here on the floor. If being short-staffed means our patients do not get the care they deserve, why should I even practice here?"

Dr. Z's comments did not go unnoticed. A patient's family overheard the conversation and asked to speak with the patient advocate. The following day, Dr. Z was called to the patient advocate's office and informed that a patient's family overheard his conversation about a patient's antibiotics and the unit being short-staffed, and they are concerned about the quality of care at the hospital. In fact, they asked the attending physician this morning if their mother could be transferred to another hospital across town.

As Chief of Staff, I was informed of this matter later in the afternoon. As I was handed the formal complaint, I opened the sealed envelope and began reading, silently:

Our mother is a patient here in this hospital, and we heard a doctor yesterday afternoon yelling at a nurse for not giving a medication on time. He said the hospital doesn't have enough nurses to take good care of the patients. My family is very concerned.

"Great," I thought to myself shaking my head in disbelief. I immediately called the patient advocate's office and asked for the phone number of the patient's daughter.

I dialed the number, and when she picked up, I said, "Hello, Mary. Are you the daughter of June, who is a patient here at the hospital?

"Yes, I am," she replied.

I immediately said, "I am Dr. Mazurek. I am the chief of staff at the hospital. I understand you have a concern with one of our physicians that you overheard yesterday. Can you tell me what happened?"

I let Mary speak without interruption. "Well," she said, "I was up in my mother's room in the early afternoon when I heard a doctor yelling at a nurse about some medicine the patient needed and had not yet received. The nurse told him the charge nurse was at a code blue, and he then yelled again about the hospital not having enough nurses to take care of patients. My mom was shocked. I was shocked. He was angry and made it seem like what we heard was a big problem all the time. I really thought about asking my mom's doctor if we could take her across town to the other hospital. We decided not to because my mom is getting better and might go home tomorrow."

I replied, "Mary, first, please accept my apologies. I am deeply sorry you had to witness a doctor behave and say things that made you and your mother rightfully feel concerned and upset. I can assure you I will be addressing your concerns with this physician, and this will not happen again. Is there anything we can do at this time?"

When she said she had no other needs, I added, "Mary, thank you for bringing up your concerns. If we are not made aware of what you heard, then it makes our job more difficult to make our hospital a better place for care. I hope your mother continues to get well."

As I hung up the phone, I realized the task at hand was straightforward.

I sent an e-mail to the other Professional Behavior Committee members regarding scheduling a meeting for the following week. Once confirmed, I called Dr. Z and briefly explained that a patient filed a formal complaint about his conduct on the floor and that we needed to have a meeting to discuss what occurred. Reluctantly, Dr. Z said he could attend.

I asked the meeting participants to arrive 30 minutes prior to the start to discuss this case and the previous complaints in this physician's file. As the meeting participants arrived, I handed each a file that included information about 15 complaints filed over a three-year period. In each case, the disposition from the Chair of Surgery was "collegial intervention, no further intervention at this time." After each member had a chance to read the file and disposition reports, I stated, "As the new Chair, I want to address the lack of escalation of consequences from these prior complaints. Regardless of what this physician states today, we have a duty and responsibility to address these past concerns and the current one in the disposition." Everyone nodded in agreement.

Dr. Z arrived, obviously irritated, sat down, and leaned back with a can of soda. Before introductions or even a welcome, he blurted, "Well, I am here. I read the complaint. This hospital sucks. If the administration would adequately staff this place, patients would be taken care of. How many times do I have to go to administration, which is completely incompetent, and tell them delays in care are harming my patients? If there is an infection or bad outcome, they get the blame, not me. And now I have to attend this b******t meeting to address a patient's family who complained about *me*? I read the complaint. Their concerns are *my concerns*. They have not been addressed for years and they continue unaddressed. I get to be the target for the hospital's problems. I get it. Someone has to take the heat for this."

I did not expect the meeting to start this way. When a meeting begins like this, the usual scripts fail. This was a complicated case with many problems contributing to the current situation. Although it was tempting to agree with the physician about the ward being short-staffed, that was not the point of the meeting. The physician essentially hijacked the meeting and set the tone. I had to reset the tone.

"Dr. Z," I stated with a deadpan face that expressed little emotion, "I realize you are frustrated with staffing and the care the patients receive. That is a topic for another discussion with the other committees and administration within the hospital. We are here today to discuss the events from last week with the patient and her family and what you stated publicly. We have a duty and responsibility to professionally communicate our concerns through proper means. Stating the hospital delivers substandard care publicly only exacerbates the problem and creates a negative and toxic environment. The committee members have looked at your file and examined the other complaints and resolutions with the Chair of Surgery, Dr. K. After numerous 'collegial discussions,' your behavior is unchanged. In one of them, you state, in front of a patient, 'I will take great care of you. I don't always trust the staff, but I will make sure things go right.'" I continued, "In most of the complaints, you make disparaging remarks about the quality of care in the hospital in front of staff and patients. You do not seem happy to work here."

Dr. Z quickly responded, "Well, I cannot leave this hospital or city. My daughter is in high school here, and my plan is to move in a couple of years.

Nothing will ever change around here, and you and the so-called committees can have all the meetings you want. If the administration is unwilling to hire enough nurses or, at the very least, really address the problems around here, it is a complete waste of everyone's time. We have had three CEOs in five years. I am sure everyone will sit down, and the new CEO will make the same b******t promises about providing great care. Everyone is looking out for their own skin."

One of the committee members quickly chimed in, "Jim, I have known you for a few years, and everyone in this hospital knows you are a great surgeon and get a lot of referrals for care. We acknowledge your concerns about staffing, and we can address that separately. But you know and I know making comments about the care in the hospital in front of patients is bad form. It is. There is no other way to spin it."

Dr. Z responded, "So, all of you agree there is an issue?"

"We will look into it," I replied, "but getting back to your behavior, you alone are responsible for your actions and must take ownership of what you said. That is why we are here. Do you understand this?"

Incredulous, Dr. Z, a bit red-faced with anger, said, "I wouldn't be here if the hospital did its f*****g job!"

And with this, the temperature of the room hit its peak level, but I said what needed to be said in front of the physician and the committee.

When encounters or meetings get overheated, you need to maintain your own emotional composure, and it is hard to do in these situations. Check yourself and breathe, however hard it might be. It is amazing what a deep breath will do for yourself.

After a few moments of awkward silence, another committee member said, "Jim, we will address the issues, and I think you know what you said was not right. That is the point of this discussion."

Dr. Z sat stone-faced and silent. He had nothing more to say or add. He shrugged his shoulders and took a sip of his soda. There really wasn't anything more he needed to say.

I spoke up. "Unless anyone else has anything to ask, Dr. Z can be excused. Jim," I stated, "we need to deliberate and discuss this event privately, and you will receive a certified letter from me in a couple of days. Thanks for coming. We all know you are upset. These meetings are not conducted to punish physicians, and I know you are unhappy."

He got up and walked out without saying a word.

After he left, we got back to the root of Dr. Z's original tirade. Why, exactly, had the patient not received the antibiotic within the timeframe as ordered per policy? This was a patient safety issue, and if staffing issues were part of the problem, this needed to be addressed. This highlights the complexity of patient safety, environment, and physician conduct.

Had the antibiotic been administered in a timely fashion, the physician would not have been angry, but this physician had a history of stating his unhappiness with the hospital. The physician looked for and identified problems to confirm this long-held belief. From the outset of the meeting, any discussions about his personal life affecting work would have been met with rejection or hostility. I sensed this.

The committee concluded the physician needed a formal letter of concern clearly stating that another event would result in a formal meeting in front of the Medical Executive Committee. We also agreed we would investigate the issue of the antibiotic administration, and I would draft a formal letter to the Patient Care Quality and Safety Committee Chair. Though not formally tasked with investigating this concern, it is within the purview of a Professional Behavior Committee to address concerns regarding patient safety if warranted. I then drafted two letters.

Letters in Response

Dr. John J.   April 5, 2014
Chair, Patient Care Quality and Safety Committee
St. Anywhere Hospital

Dear Dr. J:

The Professional Behavior Committee met with a member of the medical staff who had a concern with the proper timing of antibiotic administration for a septic patient. Information regarding the date, time, and patient ID number is located in the administrative office. We believe this event had the potential to negatively impact patient care. The medical staff member stated that the ward is short-staffed, and this may have contributed to the delay. If staffing concerns were a contributing factor, I believe we should convene a special meeting of the MEC for discussion. Thank you for taking the time to look into this matter. If you have any questions, please do not hesitate to ask me.

Kindest regards,

Matt Mazurek, MD
Chair, Professional Behavior Committee
St. Anywhere Hospital

Dear Dr. Z:

Thank you for attending the Professional Behavior Committee meeting on April 3. We certainly recognize your frustrations regarding the care of the patient and have formally addressed these issues with the Patient Care Quality and Safety Committee. That said, physicians are responsible for professional conduct and communication at all times and especially in public settings.

The patients deserve to be cared for in a respectful environment regardless of our personal opinions or concerns, and there are more effective means to communicate your concerns. You have a long history of providing conscientious, excellent care at St. Anywhere Hospital, but you are expected to conduct yourself professionally at all times. Any future conduct concerns reported by staff may lead to suspension of privileges. Please do not hesitate to contact me with any questions.

Sincerely,

Matt Mazurek, MD, MHA, CPE
Chair, Professional Behavior Committee

Case 4: He Will Not Answer His Pager

"I've paged him three times already," the circulating nurse told me.

"Well, I've had this patient on the table for about 50 minutes with a spinal, and there is only so much time left before it will start wearing off," I replied. "Last week, two of my colleagues had to convert to a general anesthetic as the spinal's anesthetic effects started wearing off during the case."

Not only was the surgeon not answering his pager, but he was also often late to arrive in the morning, frequently had a bad attitude, and treated the nurses and other staff with disrespect. Not only was his lack of professional decorum a problem, but his clinical outcomes were also impacted with complications and post-operative infections. Today's event was the last straw, and I intended to ensure the patients would receive better care from this point forward.

Rather than going through the usual processes, I confronted the surgeon privately in the sub sterile room when he arrived.

"Dr. H," I said, "this is the last time you can ignore your pages to the OR and compromise patient care. From this point forward, I have instructed my staff to not place the spinals in our patients until you are present in the OR. I am certain this will slow down your day, but I can no longer compromise patient care because you refuse to answer your pager and get your cases underway on time."

He turned beet red, and I could see him become visibly angry with me. All he said in a quick reply was, " We'll see about that." As he stormed off to the scrub sink in a huff, I thought to myself, "You cooked your own goose."

I have to admit this case definitely got the better of me. Did I let my emotions play a role in my response? You bet. I was not the Chief of Surgery, who knew about most of these behaviors and frankly was not doing his job enforcing policy. I had a problem with a disengaged Chief of Surgery and a surgeon who was running roughshod over staff and affecting patient care. I had had enough over the past three months and decided to do what I could.

When a physician's behavior directly impacts the course of care and potentially compromises patient care, it is a line in the sand. I did not have time or patience to wait for the system or anyone else responsible to intervene. I delayed placing the spinal for the next case until the surgeon entered the room. Once he entered, I placed the spinal, and what transpired next was nothing short of unconscionable. He left the room and refused to return. We waited 40 minutes. I asked the nurse to file a formal complaint to the CMO, and I drafted a formal letter to the CMO that evening.

Letter to the Attributed Physician

Dear Dr. S:

Regrettably, I am writing a formal letter of concern regarding the recent actions of Dr. H. Today, while I was performing anesthesia for his patients, Dr. H refused to answer repeated pages to let him know the patient was ready for surgery. Last week two of my colleagues had to convert and change anesthetic plans on two patients — one of whom had significant pulmonary problems that were exacerbated when we converted to general anesthesia from a spinal.

Dr. H's behavior is unnecessarily compromising patient care and placing them at risk for complications or poor outcomes. The medical staff bylaws and rules and regulations specifically address pager response times and surgeon availability once a patient is in the room. Dr. H has a pattern of engaging in these behaviors that have thus far gone unaddressed, as they continue.

I took matters into my own hands and refused to place the spinal for his second and third patients until Dr. H was present and ready. After I placed the spinal in the second case, he left the room and did not return for 40 minutes. As we were closing the case, the patient required narcotics and other pain medications we usually do not require.

I have instructed my staff to not place spinals in his patients until he is present, and if he leaves the room, to formally mark time of departure, efforts to communicate, and time of return. We will not participate in compromising patient care, and any efforts made to undermine our efforts by Dr. H will no longer be tolerated. Again, I apologize that circumstances have brought us to this point, but we have no other options than to bring these concerns to your attention.

If you have any questions or need any other information, please do not hesitate to contact me.

Most respectfully,

Matt Mazurek, MD, MHA, CPE, FASA
Chair, Department of Anesthesia

The day after he received the letter, the CMO called me into his office to discuss the situation. I was direct and to the point. There was no way to put a positive spin on the situation. I reported that no one seems to know where he goes or what he does or why he will not answer his pager. Furthermore, I said it is not my responsibility to enforce the bylaws, and the Chief of Surgery appears to be ignoring the issue, as I knew for a fact other nurses had filed more than a dozen complaints in the previous three months. I reiterated that Dr. H's behavior crossed the line when patient care is compromised. The CMO thanked me for my concerns and input.

By the next week, Dr. H's behavior changed, and for a couple of months, there was improvement. However, as I learned from comments nurses made between cases, he continued to treat the staff poorly.

Dr. H was fired a month later. The CMO shared with me that the surgeon used inappropriate language with the staff and was offered one final chance by agreeing to attend a professional program offsite, which he refused to do. In the CMO's words, there was no other alternative.

This physician exhibited all of the classic signs and symptoms of an anti-social personality disorder. His lack of empathy, creation of conflict, and blatant disregard of his actions impacting patient care support this diagnosis. The surgeon left the area and opened a new practice, which failed nine months later. He moved to another state and joined a group but was terminated after one year. I doubt this physician will recognize his own issues were the primary cause for these terminations.

PHYSICAL AGGRESSION AND ASSAULT

There is extensive literature on bullying in healthcare. These cases present the unusual circumstances of either threatened or actual physical violence against people or objects. Physical assault is a crime. In my opinion, a physician who has been charged with and found guilty of assault should be terminated. At the end of this section, I briefly discuss the prevalence and incidence of horizontal violence.

Case 1: Should I Call the Police?

Cesare Pavese, a famous Italian poet, once said, "We do not remember days, we remember moments." And never was this truer than on a warm, sunny July day as my family and I piled into a minivan with another family on our way to Rocky Mountain National Park a few years ago. I was on vacation and was not expecting any communication regarding concerns at the hospital. I was recently appointed as Chief of Staff, Elect and Chair of Professional Behavior. I had been in this position for only five days. As Chair of Anesthesia, I had investigated a few professional conduct complaints within my own department of 40 plus members over a six-year span. Now, I was responsible for over 600 medical staff.

Over the hum of the tires, and the kids singing "The Wheels on the Bus," I heard my phone ring. It was Marge, our Chief Nursing Officer.

"Matt, I know you are on vacation, and I know you just took over as Chair of Professional Behavior, but we have a situation here you need to know about."

Somewhat surprised, I replied, "Yes, go ahead."

"Dr. W lost control and was yelling and screaming at a nurse outside the ICU, and he seemed to be physically threatening her. A patient's family member, concerned and shocked at what was happening, asked if they should call the police."

"Call the police?" I asked.

"Yes," Marge said emphatically.

"Is there any other doc available to cover the rest of Dr. W's shift?"

Marge replied quickly, "Yes, one of his partners is coming in to complete his shift. The nurse is pretty shaken by this, and we sent her home as well."

As a physician leader, I am always available for "big" problems. It's a small price to pay for peace of mind, and I would rather know about an issue and consequences before I arrive on a Monday morning and get blindsided. I have never had to ask anyone, "Why didn't you call?" After years of leadership, I can separate and compartmentalize these issues as they arrive.

I asked Marge if there was anything else that needed to be done, and she replied that everything was under control. She assured me that if anything came up, she would call me. I thanked her for letting me know, hung up the phone, and for the next 30 minutes thought about the scene that must have transpired. As the mountain peaks rose higher and higher in the windshield, I slowly forgot about the call and moved on — knowing I could take care of it next week.

When I returned to the hospital, I immediately asked for the report from the ICU charge RN and the RN who was threatened. This, unfortunately, was not this physician's first incident. There were three prior events involving verbal abuse, name-calling, and angry, uncontrolled outbursts. This latest incident, which included physical posturing suggesting a threat to hit or shove the nurse, was an escalation in the behavior. As I read many of the prior reports and dispositions, and I discovered a history of treatment for alcohol use disorder a couple of years ago. I wondered if the physician was once again using alcohol.

This incident prompted a request for the Professional Behavior Committee to convene within 72 hours. I also notified the physician that a meeting would be scheduled and informed him that, given the nature of the complaint, we needed to discuss the incident immediately. Workplace violence combined with a history of alcohol use is a combination that can lead to another event with dire consequences. There was, undoubtedly, a lot at stake.

At the meeting, after brief introductions, I recounted the events from the prior week and asked Dr. W for his perspective. He was normally a good-natured person and easy to talk to, but he did have a tendency to quickly change from calm to visibly upset within a minute.

He replied, "I remember what happened that day. I was post-call and had been on-call for three days without sleep. I had put in some orders early in the morning for the patient to be transferred to the floor. I was once again on-call and had another admit from the ER, but I was told there was no room in the ICU. The patient was very unstable and required pressors for blood pressure support. I didn't want the patient to sit in the ER. The house supervisor then called me and said there was a discharge order for the patient from the ICU to the floor, but the nurse had not acknowledged receiving it and didn't know it was placed. I walked over to the unit and asked the nurse why she wasn't looking at the orders I had already placed. She gave me a flippant excuse that she had another patient not doing well. I guess I got angry."

I replied, "Yes, you got angry enough for a patient's family to be concerned about calling the police. This is pretty serious."

I then asked an open-ended question, "How are you doing?"

"Well," he said, "I am tired. I am very tired. I have been doing call two weeks at a time on and off for several months. I get called all night long and do admits. I go home and crash after dinner, get up at 6 a.m. and do this day after day without a day off. I was in my second week when this happened."

"Dr. W," I said, "you have a history of a problem with alcohol, and I know you have been in treatment in the past. I know this is a sensitive question, but have you been drinking again?"

Dr. W replied, "No, I have been sober for a couple of years — since treatment. I am just really tired."

I invited other committee members to ask questions.

Dr. A asked, "Why are you working such an odd schedule without a day off? Your schedule is worse than most residents who are doing ICU fellowships."

"There are only two of us covering the ICU right now," Dr. W answered. "You know we have an open unit, so some of the surgeons and hospitalists follow their patients in the ICU. All other patients are assigned to us. I typically only have 8 to 10 patients per day, but sometimes I have to discharge 3 or 4 and then get 3 admits — typically in the afternoon. It is a lot. I know it. And I am tired."

Everyone nodded in agreement.

I said, "Dr. W, I think you are overworked and exhausted. You need to take time off and take care of yourself. In the meantime, you must recognize the seriousness of the perception that you were threatening a nurse with assault through your body language and tone of voice. This cannot happen. We are here to support and help you. Is there anything we can do for you?"

Dr. W replied, "I just need to work less. I will see what I can do."

I excused him from the meeting, and the committee members discussed the disposition of the case. All agreed he needed to get rest, but we also recommended an anger management course, as there was a history of prior events involving angry outbursts.

Letter to the Attributed Physician

Dear Dr. W:

Thank you for taking the time to meet with the Professional Behavior Committee on July 10, 2021. We appreciate how hard you work to provide care for the patients at St. Anywhere and know you are committed to doing a great job. As you stated in the meeting, you know you are working too many days in a row on-call to give yourself time for adequate rest. This contributed to events on July 5, and we are concerned your lack of rest might also compromise patient care.

As physicians, we have a responsibility to communicate respectfully with all support staff and RNs. Your behavior on July 5 was perceived as threatening — verbally and physically. Therefore, we recommend you complete a course with coaching, at your expense, on managing your emotional response to situations and reducing angry outbursts. You have two months to complete this course, and you can attend either an in-person or online course. We have provided a list of possible programs you can choose.

Failure to complete the course in the given timeframe may jeopardize your privileges. Furthermore, if there are any more events where staff feels threatened, you may also lose your privileges. We value your care here at St. Anywhere, and we are here to support you, but ultimately, you are responsible for your behavior and actions. Thank you again for your time. If you have any concerns or questions, please do not hesitate to contact me or a member of the Professional Behavior Committee. We recognize the sensitive nature of the incident and will respectfully keep these discussions and matter confidential.

Kind regards,

Matthew Mazurek, MD, MHA, CPE, FASA
Chair, Professional Behavior Committee

For the remainder of my tenure in my position, Dr. W no longer had any other issues. After I left my position, I heard there was another incident involving an RN. The physician was employed by one of the large national staffing companies, and the company exercised the right to terminate the physician for cause.

Case 2: Operating Room Rage

The door hung on a twisted hinge outside OR 4; crumbled bits of broken glass were strewn across the floor. Moments earlier, a surgeon had angrily slammed the door so hard it hit the wall and shattered the tiny window. The surgeon stomped off in a huff, over the shards of glass, rounded the corner, and walked down the hall. It all happened so fast the staff stood by in disbelief. This was the latest event in a series of inappropriate behaviors.

Dr. H had a reputation for being incredibly rude and condescending to nearly all staff members — especially in the OR. Today was different, as his frustrations led to the physical destruction of property. It was an aggressive, violent outburst. Although I did not witness the event, I confirmed the details from numerous sources, including one of my colleagues in the anesthesia department. I was not surprised an event like this occurred.

After documenting the event, my colleague, Dr. B, and I were asked to discuss the incident with the CMO. We were briefed on the confidentiality of the conversation, and I nodded my head in agreement, then emphasized to my colleague that what we said and heard in the meeting was confidential. The OR environment is always rich with gossip, and events like this generate a lot of buzz and curiosity.

Dr. W, the CMO, opened the meeting: "So, Dr. B, can you explain what happened in OR 2 on Thursday?"

"Well," Dr. B replied, "we were finishing the case and closing the wound, and everything seemed to be going fine. The case went smoothly, and other than the usual complaints from Dr. H, it was just another day in the OR. About halfway through the wound closure, the suture snapped and broke, and Dr. H stuck himself in the thumb or finger. He jumped off the chair, tore off his gloves and gown while yelling at the nurses about the broken suture. Without any warning, he opened the door, and slammed it against the wall. The glass shattered, and the door handle left a small dent in the wall."

"Is there anything more you would like to add?"

Dr. B. quickly shared, "I am not at all surprised Dr. H did this. He has a tendency to be quite rude, yells at OR nurses, and seems angry. No one in our group wants to work with him, and I know we share the burden of working with him among all of the staff. He arrives late after we have placed spinals for our total joint patients, and on more than one occasion, the anesthesiologist has had to convert to a general anesthetic because the spinal started to wear off. It frankly sucks to be in his room."

"Thank you for sharing this information with me today," Dr. W replied. We were dismissed without any further comments. A couple of months later, the physician was terminated.

In a similar vein, two physicians in Ohio were arguing over the medical management of a patient. One physician accused the other of "going behind his back" to continue administering the medication. While arguing, the accused physician asked the other to lower his voice. The incident escalated to the point where one physician shoved the other and a nurse and staff member had to intervene.[10] The physician was arrested and charged with assault.

VIOLENCE IN THE HEALTHCARE SETTING

Horizontal violence (HV) in the healthcare setting is a problem. An interesting study examined HV occurrence among emergency physicians, residents, and physician assistants.[11] Unfortunately, physicians and HV occurrence is not well studied, yet there are numerous studies on the subject in nursing literature. Nearly one-quarter of the participants in a survey of nurses felt

HV affected patient care; some participants indicated they believed a few purposely intended to "do harm."[12]

Prevention efforts include providing education during training to raise awareness of HV. Other initiatives include examining the healthcare organization's structure, work environment, policies, and normative behaviors. Healthcare organizations operate under the culture and behaviors they tolerate. In response, some organizations have instituted zero-tolerance policies with mixed results.[13] In conclusion, there is a pressing need to find out innovative, creative solutions to the problem.

DRUG DIVERSION AND IMPAIRMENT

Substance use disorder impacts both the physician and his or her patients with potentially devastating consequences, and further discussion on this important topic is provided in Chapter 10. Mishandling or inappropriately storing controlled substances is a serious matter. The following case describes one of these instances.

Case 1: Missing Drugs

Drug diversion and substance use disorder (SUD) is a problem for many physicians who have easy access to controlled substances. Anesthesiologists, especially, are prone to succumbing to opioid addiction. Substance use disorder in anesthesiologists is estimated to be between 1-2%. It certainly is not a common problem, but this level of prevalence translates to several hundred anesthesiologists with the disorder. A majority of anesthesiologists with SUD are younger than 35, part of academic programs, and have a strong history of SUD and/or alcohol use disorder in the family.[14]

Years ago, one of my colleagues was reported to the DEA for improperly possessing and storing narcotic medications at his home. To protect his anonymity, I cannot divulge all of the details other than the fact his spouse reported the cache. Once I was made aware of this, his privileges to practice were immediately suspended, and a report to the medical board was filed.

I had two immediate concerns related to this event. First, I was concerned there may be a SUD problem; he was referred for drug testing. Fortunately, the results were negative. Second, I wondered if this purposeful diversion was for illegal distribution or sale. Fortunately, after interviews and investigations from the DEA and medical staff leadership, it was determined that this, too, was not the case.

What transpired seems innocent on the surface. In our practice, anesthesiologists removed opioids and controlled substances for cases on an individual basis. For example, if I provided care for a patient for gall bladder surgery, I personally obtained the narcotics I thought I would need for the case. In the event I did not use the medications, I could return them to the pharmacy dispensing machines with a witness. Late at night while on call, it was easy to forget we had the unused medications, as we stored them in our front pockets. Many times, the medications were discovered at home, unopened. Most of us had the habit of returning the medications the following day. This physician simply tossed the unopened medications in a drawer at the bedside.

Another problem with this case was billable fraud. The medications are assigned to a patient and case. If not returned, the patient and insurance are charged. The cache was sizeable — dozens of vials. It was impossible to trace and reconcile the discrepancies and charges. Additionally, having possession was also theft.

Although after six months of investigation from the DEA and hospital leadership, the physician was found not guilty of any crimes or of having SUD, the physician still had to report to the Medical Executive Committee for a special session and disposition. At the meeting, the physician was remorseful, apologetic, and understood the seriousness of the circumstances. Collectively, we thanked him for his time, excused him from the meeting, and opened the floor for discussion. There was unanimous opinion that the physician simply had a lapse in judgment and he should be allowed to return to practice.

Mishandling narcotics or any controlled substances is a consistent problem in most hospitals. Nurses personally administer a majority of the drugs in a hospital setting, and there are processes and procedures in place to properly handle any waste or unused drugs.

Case 2: The Impaired Physician

It was 11:00 am on a late October Wednesday when I received the phone call. As Chair of Anesthesia, I was used to daily calls for various reasons. This was different. When I picked up the phone, our OR director said, "Dr.

Mazurek we have a problem in OR 6. The charge nurse says Dr. B is falling asleep behind the drape. Can you come in to see what's going on?"

I was certainly alarmed and wanted to immediately evaluate what was taking place, but was in the middle of my own case and had no one to relieve me.

I asked, "Is the patient OK and surgeon aware?"

"Yes," she replied.

"I will get out as soon as possible," I said.

Approximately 45 minutes later, I was relieved from my case and encountered Dr. B in the hallway. He was done with the case and stumbling down the hall, ataxic with bloodshot eyes. I thought to myself, "He's drunk."

"Hey John. How are you doing? Would you care to come into my office for a minute?" I asked.

"Sure," he said.

"Mary, the OR director called me during your last case and shared a concern with me. She says the charge nurse thought you might be falling asleep behind the drape. Did you get any sleep last night?" I asked.

He slurred, "I haven't been getting much sleep."

"Well, I have to relieve you of duty," I informed him, "and you must go to employee health for an evaluation."

"I cannot do that," he replied.

When I asked him why he couldn't do that, he replied, "Because I just can't. I am going to go home now."

Before I could react, he hurriedly left, heading toward the parking lot and ignoring my requests to stop. I realized my colleague had just performed an anesthetic while impaired and now was driving impaired. The events of this day remain seared into my memory.

That evening, after another partner sat down with him and discussed his options, he wisely checked into a treatment and recovery center. Unfortunately, this was strike two. Several years prior, he had been drinking on-call, although he did not provide any clinical care. He was offered the chance to enter a treatment program, which he successfully completed.

Unknown to many of us, he began drinking again after the probationary period ended. None of us had recognized the signs of his impairment during the first episode. Physicians are more prone to alcoholism than the general population simply because of the stress and nature of the work. It is estimated 10-15% of physicians have an alcohol problem, including binge drinking, abuse, or alcoholism. Estimating the prevalence of alcoholism in physicians is difficult, but even if we assume the rate is like the general population, this remains a huge problem.[15]

Dr. B left the second round of treatment after 60 days, moved to another state, and started drinking heavily again. He was arrested for a DUI, and one year later, we learned of his passing. His death has haunted me for several years. My colleagues and I often wonder what we could have done to prevent this tragedy.

Ultimately, we are all responsible for our own behavior, but impaired physicians need life-long treatment and monitoring. Our current system needs to recognize addiction as a disease, and it especially needs to recognize that physicians should not be punished but treated with compassion in a system supporting these facts. I will always remember Dr. B as a young, exceptionally bright, and talented colleague who fell ill with addiction.

PASSIVE BEHAVIOR

Passive behaviors can be very disruptive to the workflow environment in the clinical setting. Poor communication or complete lack of communication and delays in charting creates chaos. The case presented here is a common problem for some physicians: incomplete charting. Incomplete charting can create a problem if a patient requires a higher level of care or presents to the emergency department and the prior clinic visit note is not complete. The scenarios and situations are countless.

An additional impact is the financial cost of delayed billing and charges. Delays directly impact the financial health of the organization. Some institutions have provided small bonus incentives for physicians to complete charts in a timely manner. Lastly, timely documentation is a part of many medical staff rules and regulations or bylaws. If a physician continues to be delinquent, a temporary suspension of privileges may be your only option.

Case 1: A Mountain of Unfinished Charts

Dr. M stared blankly at the screen. His inbox contained more than 289 unread messages, 35 incomplete charts, and 15 open charts that were not dictated from patient visits six days ago. This backlog impacted timely insurance billing and incomplete charts affected patient care, as two of the patients were recently hospitalized after the clinic visits, but no updates on treatment were documented from the clinic, which delayed treatment. Efforts to help the physician complete the charts failed, and the physician was upset when the old paper chart system was replaced by, in his words, "a god-awful computer."

Every organization has a token few physicians who are sloppy or delay completing documentation. In some cases, the physician is both sloppy and tardy. Professionalism expectations include timely and accurate completion of patient charts.

Dr. M had many opportunities to improve his performance, and it was appropriate to elevate the concern to the committee level. I set up a meeting with the other members of the Professional Behavior Committee and called Dr. M to ask when he could meet with the committee. Dr. M is an agreeable, approachable physician. In fact, his patients seek his care, and he has an excellent bedside manner. I knew he would be receptive to a phone call.

"Hey Matt, what can I do for you?" he asked when he answered my call.

"Jim, I hope your day is going well, and I wish I wasn't put in this position to have to call you, but the Professional Behavior Committee needs to meet with you about your charting."

"OK," he replied. "When do you want to meet? I have clinic most afternoons until 4 p.m. I can make a 4:30 p.m. meeting Monday through Thursday."

I scheduled the meeting with the committee for the following Tuesday, and as everyone gathered prior, we briefly discussed the issue. Everyone seemed to agree there was a time management/workflow concern. Dr. M arrived, and after some formal introductions, I showed Dr. M the bylaws explaining timely completion of charts.

"Jim," I said, "we have had several discussions regarding incomplete charts and the mountain of unfinished charts in your inbox. We want to help you, but first, we must understand why you are not meeting expectations."

"Well," Dr. M replied, "I spend a lot of time with my patients and pay attention to them one-on-one, of course, and I take notes in shorthand as I go throughout the day. I used to have an assistant who would take my shorthand, translate my notes, and put them in the paper chart. That is gone now that there is an electronic medical record. My assistant struggles with organizing my notes. I struggle with knowing what to do as well. The EMR sucks."

"I understand," I said. What if we get a super user to assist you in creating some templates or creating a workflow in the EMR you can use to keep up with documentation throughout the day? Does this sound reasonable?"

Dr. M agreed to get in-person assistance from a super user and the IT department, and after a couple of months, charts were completed on time and documentation was complete.

This case highlights the fact that the behavior was not intentional, and though he could have asked for help, he chose to simply suffer through the misery on his own. Not all of the professional meetings you conduct will be mired in conflict or unpleasant conversations. Sometimes there is an easy fix.

PATIENT COMPLAINT

Patients have a right to respectful treatment in a professional environment. When a family or patient witnesses hostile or unprofessional conduct, trust and confidence are lost. Directly or indirectly insulting patients is never warranted. When a patient reports unprofessional conduct or a concern, we must be objective and gather all facts. Occasionally, cultural misunderstandings or miscommunication is the issue, and in some cases, patients who are under the influence of drugs or alcohol literally impairs their judgment.

Case 1: The Doctor Told Me I Am Fat

"A word is dead when it is said, some say. I say it just begins to live that day."
—*Emily Dickinson*

Dr. S in pre-op Room 4 smiled and said, "Hello, are you Janet Johnson, the patient of Dr. Jones, the surgeon?" The patient nodded. "Yes," and Dr. S quickly said, "I will be your anesthesiologist for your gallbladder surgery today."

I was patiently waiting in the nurse's station for my surgeon to arrive as my partner continued with the dialogue across the hall. "Well, Janet, do you have sleep apnea?"

Janet responded, "Why yes, I have sleep apnea and was told to bring my machine. It is in a case under the chair over in the corner. I use it nightly, and it really helps a lot."

Dr. S said, "You know, Janet, your sleep apnea would probably go away if you weren't so fat. Your BMI is 37. Has your primary care doctor asked you about any methods you can use to lose some weight?"

Janet's eyes widened and she was obviously shocked and upset, as was her husband, who sat quietly in the corner.

"Yes, I have tried multiple times, but I am on prednisone and have been taking it for years. No matter what I do, I cannot seem to lose weight," she explained. "I would exercise, but I have had three back fusions."

Dr. S replied, "I am sorry you have had such a hard time."

I thought to myself, "Here we go again." This physician already had two patient complaints.

As Chair of Professional Behavior, I had a few options, including doing nothing, writing an incident report, immediately asking the physician to speak with me privately about the matter, or waiting until day's end to write an incident report and speak with the physician and patient. I decided to wait. The damage was done, and creating a scene in front of the patient would only add fuel to the fire, as I also knew the physician would become upset and defensive.

At the end of the day, I approached the physician and explained that I had witnessed the entire pre-operative evaluation from the nurse's station just across the hall and had overheard the conversation. I quickly explained that she would have to meet with the Professional Behavior Committee to discuss today's events.

I told her that her comments were completely inappropriate and served no purpose in providing anesthesia services. I expected her to become defensive. She replied, "Well, I don't really see the problem the way you do. About half of our patients are overweight or obese, and it gets old taking care of them day after day. We are expected to provide excellent care, and it is as though they do not care about themselves. I am sick of it."

I responded, "I get that you are frustrated. I can hear that in your voice. But, there are more constructive ways for you to manage your frustrations. First, you are not alone. All of us struggle with the same issues. Unfortunately, our particular career choice means we have to manage difficult airways and obese patients professionally and safely. We are here to help each other out, and if you need help, you can always ask one of us for a second pair of hands."

The following week, Dr. S sat with the committee. First, I asked the committee members to introduce themselves as she was only casually acquainted with some of them. I thanked Dr. S for the many years of service she has provided and then showed her copies of the signed professional conduct form. The document explicitly states patients are to be treated with compassionate, dignified, respectful care.

I asked Dr. S, "Can you please explain why you felt it necessary to say the patient was fat?"

She quickly replied, "The patient is fat, that's why, and I thought it would help, as a physician, to state this and possibly make the patient aware of how much this impacted her care. I explained to you later that day I am frustrated."

"Dr. S, I think we can all relate to your frustrations over the challenges of providing care for obese patients," I replied, "but we have a duty and responsibility to be compassionate and respectful at all times. Do you agree that a statement like this can make a patient feel hurt and disrespected?"

Dr. S said, "I guess so, but you know, and I know the patient knows the problem and probably doesn't care."

"I think it is dangerous and presumptive to assume how a patient feels about their medical conditions," I stated, surprised at her response.

I opened the floor for other committee members to ask questions or provide comments.

Dr. J stated, "I agree with Dr. Mazurek. We have a responsibility to be respectful to our patients regardless of how we feel or what we think. I am certain this patient felt insulted, and this erodes trust. Can I ask you a question?"

"Sure," Dr. S said.

"Are you stressed, or is anything in your personal life affecting how you feel at work? The reason I ask is that there have been two other complaints in the past two months."

Dr. S adjusted her chair and leaned forward, stating, "My personal life is no one's business."

A bit taken aback by this, I said, "Dr. S, the committee is not here to punish you. We are here to help physicians who may need it, and we also have a duty to ensure patients are taken care of in a respectful manner. If there are personal issues affecting physician behavior, we can assist."

"Oh, OK. Like I said, thank you, but my personal business is mine, so please do not ask again," she said.

No one else had any comments, and her tone and body language indicated she would not say anything else, so I concluded the discussion and kindly asked Dr. S to be excused.

This case was unique. I was the one who created the report, and my colleague was fully aware of this after our conversation. In retrospect, this was a mistake. The fact that I made the report and was presiding over the meeting made the physician feel especially vulnerable. From her perspective, it was difficult to know if the report was perhaps personal.

Many hospitals' bylaws and conduct codes give department chairs the authority to investigate professional conduct reports. There is an inherent problem with this process, and damaging professional relationships happens in these situations.

PHYSICIAN DENIGRATING ANOTHER PHYSICIAN

Physicians have a responsibility to instill trust in patients and the care they receive. The following case is unique, and I am certain you will conclude there was nothing of value communicated to the patient. The only motive for a physician to tell a patient another physician is providing substandard care is to boost his or her own ego. It serves no other purpose. If a patient seeks a second opinion, it's obvious they have a concern or desire more information. Telling a patient another physician is incompetent without explanation is never warranted.

Case 1: Dr. S Is Incompetent

Dr. F asked the patient, "So, Dr. S took care of you, huh?"

The patient smiled. "Yes, I love Dr. S! She was the greatest, and she made me feel relaxed the last time I was here getting surgery."

"Well," Dr. F stated, "Dr. S is not very good."

The patient was shocked to hear this statement, and so was the patient's family. They filed a formal complaint with the patient advocate, and I received notice of it a few days later. This case contains the same elements as a physician who says improper statements about the hospital or healthcare organization. Confidence and trust in the system is broken, and it is difficult to walk back the fallout from these events.

I called the patient to ask for more details about what was stated and to apologize on behalf of the organization and the department. The patient was glad I called and had wondered if there would be any follow-up. I thanked them for speaking with me and promised them they would not have another poor and unprofessional experience.

Unfortunately, this physician had a long history of poor communication and a bad attitude toward patients. There were at least four other incidents in the past three years involving patient complaints and another six or seven involving nurses and physicians from other service lines. Dr. F's demeanor was often interpreted as rude, condescending, and disrespectful. Corrective action to this point included two meetings prior to this event. These efforts failed, so as a last resort, the physician was referred to a professional coach and mandated to participate or face termination.

As this program was confidential, I was not privy to how it worked. I was told that out of 60 participants, only four failed to complete the program; one who did was subsequently terminated after the behaviors continued. Some physicians gain insight over time; some do not. If they do not, you have an obligation to move forward, as the continued behavior is unacceptable.

This case is interesting because the physician had no reason to discuss her opinion regarding prior care — especially if the patient had a positive experience. What purpose did this encounter serve? Perhaps it was cathartic release?

Later, I discuss some of the motives behind negative gossip.

It is likely this encounter made the physician feel powerful and influential. Regardless, these types of comments undermine trust and impede the provision of safe and effective care.

Case 2: Consequences of Doing Nothing

This case is interesting and unusual, and I am sharing it because it demonstrates the consequences of not doing enough. The physician leader who shared this case asked me to help guide his management of a difficult case, and I was more than happy to assist him.

My friend Dave called me one day to ask about a physician who had a long history of patient complaints about her rude and condescending tone. Dave was just hired as a chair of a small department, and the COO of the hospital had warned him of this physician. The behaviors were documented for several years. Inheriting a problem physician is a huge problem. Corrective action should have taken place prior to Dave's arrival.

I told Dave that giving the physician a pass for any new behaviors was not an option. As I pointed out in prior chapters, if a disruptive physician with a long track record of issues becomes your problem, you must act swiftly to correct the situation. I told Dave that if he allowed it to continue, then the message to the attributed physician was that nothing would happen. I told him to read all prior complaints and dispositions and let me know what he found.

Unfortunately, every disposition ended with the dreaded "collegial discussion." There was no escalation in consequences, no letters to the physician demonstrating the importance of changing the behavior, etc. After two months, another complaint from a patient was filed against the physician. He called to ask me what the next step should be. I told him now is the time to inform the physician that given the long history of prior complaints, a formal meeting is necessary to discuss the concerns.

He agreed, set up the meeting, and called me the day after the meeting. The meeting did not go well. The physician was not apologetic or conciliatory and did not seem to understand the implications and consequences. I told him that a physician who lacks insight and is unwilling to acknowledge the behavior is a big problem. I told him to document all points of discussion and write a letter warning the physician that continued events could lead to loss of privileges or termination. He sent the letter, which the physician signed and returned.

The following month another complaint was filed by an ER nurse who stated the physician was "rude" and "condescending" toward ER staff who had requested assistance with an IV start. Another meeting was scheduled, and the physician again failed to acknowledge her behavior. Another letter followed with the warning that the next complaint would lead to a meeting with the regional medical director.

The next incident involved Dave himself as the medical director. The physician was scheduled for a case, but due to a patient request for a female provider, Dave asked the physician to switch rooms. The physician refused the request. Insubordination is serious, as this behavior undermined Dave's authority. Furthermore, it impacted patient care. Dave called his regional medical director, and a formal meeting was set up to terminate the physician.

In a strange twist of events, the regional medical director and other team members chose to place the physician in a performance improvement program instead of terminating her. Dave was quite upset with this development. First, he was not involved in the decision. Second, he disagreed with the plan. Dave knew, too, that the decision was based on not wanting to leave the department short-staffed. This is a mistake many organizations make. Do not retain physicians who are problems regardless of circumstances.

Dave was present at the meeting with the physician along with a representative from the company and the regional medical director. The physician was never apologetic and never acknowledged responsibility for her actions. She signed an agreement to participate in a program with the company, and Dave was given updates from the program physician/coach. Dave remained skeptical the behavior would change. He was right.

After participating, the company that had contracted anesthesia services lost the contract. All of the physicians had to reapply for their positions within the hospital system or find employment at other locations within the company. Despite ongoing concerns, the hospital offered the physician a contract. Soon after the contract was signed, a patient filed a formal complaint against the physician for making disparaging remarks about a prior provider's care with whom the patient was pleased. The physician told the patient that the prior provider was "not very good." Dave was exasperated.

The physician continued to confront staff and make inappropriate comments and remarks. Another report was created and filed, and Dave refused to participate in any meetings with the physician, as the professional relationship had eroded to the point he felt he was not effective, that it was personal.

The physician's behavior continued and impacted staff morale. Dave told me his work environment had become toxic. He was open to new possibilities and resigned as medical director because of the failure of two organizations to do the right thing and terminate the physician. The physician remains employed.

This case highlights the need for organizations to proactively address behaviors and adhere to plans. If a physician's behavior is egregious enough to warrant termination, then the plan must remain in place regardless of local staffing needs. The decision to not terminate undermined Dave's leadership and also added a level of distrust that Dave would be supported with other decisions. Sadly, the organization lost a great physician and leader, and it was completely avoidable.

SOCIAL MEDIA PITFALLS

Social media is ubiquitous, but there are pitfalls and traps for physicians who choose to use the medium. Physicians who use social media should maintain as much privacy as possible. Do not make your pages public. Patients and colleagues can easily search your profile and discover personal information you would never share publicly.

In addition:

1. Never discuss patient care or progress or pictures on social media.
2. Be careful who you are connected with at work. If your colleagues or other medical staff have access to your content, you can assume everyone in the hospital or clinic can gain access. Your posts will feed grist to the gossip mill.
3. Do not post disparaging remarks about colleagues, the organization, patient care, etc.
4. Check your privacy settings frequently.

Be aware of the consequences of controversial posts. Nurses and physicians have been terminated for violating HIPAA rules, insulting colleagues or patients, and openly criticizing the hospitals, clinics, or systems they work for or with. It is not worth it to post anything negative. Other than brief cathartic relief, it does not create change or solve problems.

LinkedIn is the largest and most influential social media and professional networking site, and I enjoy its platform and learn a lot from fellow colleagues. Again, however, beware of posting politically controversial content not grounded in objective facts, etc. People are free to disagree on this platform, but doing so needs to be done respectfully. My rules on LinkedIn are to imagine the posts being published in a professional journal or delivered in front of a hundred of my peers.

DISRUPTIVE PHYSICIAN LEADERS

I am opening this section with a tragic case study from the United States Air Force. I include this story because disruptive physician leaders often get a "pass" due to their position of authority. Disciplining a physician in a leadership position is difficult and political. I could have shortened this story, but I think all of the details are important to demonstrate an organization can fail. Doing *nothing* is an option but doing nothing is the poorest option on the table.

It was a clear day in the state of Washington on June 24, 1994. A B-52 bomber crew led by Lt. Col. Arthur "Bud" Holland was preparing to practice at Fairchild Air Force Base for maneuvers it would perform for an upcoming airshow. Sadly, that afternoon, the B-52 crashed during a "go around" near the base.

The weather was clear and there were no mechanical issues. It was clearly pilot error that led to the fatal accident that not only killed Lt. Col. Holland but three other senior officers on board. Thankfully, no one on the ground was injured, but many family members witnessed the accident, and their lives were profoundly impacted by this event.

The series of events leading to this tragedy highlight the importance of intervention when someone in authority "breaks the rules." The story behind this story is one of an arrogant pilot who was allowed to continue to fly.

Immediately after the accident, Brigadier General Orin Godsey was given authority, as the USAF's Chief of Safety, to investigate the circumstances that led to this crash. His findings were released to the Department of Defense but not the general public. A separate investigation, called AFR-110-14, was released to the public in 1995, and the findings are disturbing.

The accident board stated that Bud Holland's personality significantly influenced the crash sequence. USAF personnel testified that Holland had developed a reputation as an aggressive pilot who often broke flight-safety and other rules.

What follows are some testimonials and stories from 1991-1994 regarding Holland's behavior and performance:[16]

1. In 1991, a B-52 piloted by Holland performed a circle above a softball game in which Holland's daughter was participating. Beginning at 2,500 feet (760 m) AGL, Holland's aircraft executed the circle at 65° of bank. In a maneuver described by one witness as a "death spiral," the nose of the aircraft continued to drop, and the bank angle increased to 80°. After losing 1,000 feet (300 m) of altitude, Holland was able to regain control of the aircraft.

2. During a May 1991 air show at Fairchild, Holland was the command pilot of the B-52 aerial-demonstration flight. During the demonstration, Holland's aircraft *violated several safety regulations,* including exceeding bank and pitch limits, flying directly over the air-show spectators, and possibly violating altitude restrictions. The base and wing commander, Colonel Arne Weinman, along with his staff, observed the demonstration, but apparently *took no action.*

3. In July 1991, Holland commanded a B-52 for a "flyover" during a change-of-command ceremony for the 325th Bomb Squadron at Fairchild. During both the practice and the actual flyover, Holland's aircraft flew at altitudes below 100 feet (30 m) – well below the established minimum altitude – flew steeply banked turns in excess of 45°, exceeded pitch-angle limits, and executed a wingover. The wingover was not specifically prohibited but was not recommended, because it could damage the aircraft. After witnessing the flyover, Colonel Weinman and his deputy commander for operations (DO), Colonel Julich, *orally reprimanded Holland, but took no formal action.*

4. During the May 1992 Fairchild air show, Holland was again the command pilot of the B-52 aerial-demonstration flight. During the demonstration, Holland's aircraft again *violated several safety regulations,* including several low-altitude, steep turns in excess of 45° of bank and a high pitch angle climb, estimated at over 60° nose high which Holland finished with a wingover maneuver. The new wing commander, Colonel Michael G. Ruotsala, apparently *took no action.* One week later, the new DO, Colonel Capotosti, on his own initiative, warned Holland that if he violated any more safety regulations, Capotosti would ground him (remove him from flying status). Capotosti *did not document his warning to Holland or take any other kind of formal action.*

5. In April 1993, Holland was the mission commander of a two-ship training mission to a bombing range near Guam in the Pacific Ocean. During the mission, *Holland flew his B-52 closer to the other B-52 than regulations allowed.* Holland also asked his navigator to videotape the bombs falling from the aircraft from inside the bomb bay, also against regulations. Holland's navigator later brought the video to the attention of three Fairchild USAF officers. The first, Lieutenant Colonel

Bullock, the current 325th Bomb Squadron commander, did not do anything about it and may have even tried to use the videotape as leverage to coerce the navigator into accepting a position as mission scheduler for the wing. The second, the deputy operations group commander, Lieutenant Colonel Harper, told the crew member to *conceal the evidence.* The third, the DO, allegedly responded to reports of the video by stating, "Okay, I don't want to know anything about that video — I don't care."

6. At the August 1993 Fairchild air show, Holland once again commanded the B-52 demonstration flight. The demonstration profile once again included bank angles greater than 45°, low-altitude passes, and another high pitch climbing maneuver, this time in excess of 80° nose high. The climb was so steep that fuel flowed out of the vent holes from the aircraft's wing tanks. The new wing commander, Brigadier General James M. Richards, and the new DO, Colonel William E. Pellerin, both witnessed the demonstration, but *neither took any action.*

7. In March 1994, Holland commanded a single-aircraft training mission to the Yakima Bombing Range, to provide an authorized photographer an opportunity to document the aircraft as it dropped training munitions. *The minimum aircraft altitude permitted for that area was 500 feet* (150 m) AGL. During the mission, Holland's aircraft was filmed crossing one ridgeline about *30 feet* (10 m) above the ground. *Fearing for their safety, the photography crew ceased filming and took cover as Holland's aircraft again passed low over the ground, this time estimated as clearing the ridge line by only three feet (1 m).* The co-pilot on Holland's aircraft testified that he grabbed the controls to prevent Holland from flying the aircraft into the ridge while the aircraft's other two aircrew members repeatedly screamed at Holland: "Climb! Climb!" —(*these accounts are taken from Wikipedia.*)

8. *The last event was the crash on June 24, 1994.* The accident investigation concluded that the crash was primarily attributable to Holland's personality and behavior, USAF leaders' inadequate reactions to the previous incidents involving Holland, and the sequence of events and aircrew response during the final flight of the aircraft. Holland's disregard for procedures governing the safe operation of the B-52

aircraft that he commanded and the absence of firm and consistent corrective action by his superior officers allowed Holland to believe he could conduct his flight in an unsafe manner, culminating with the slow, steeply banked, 360° turn around the control tower.

But there is far more to this story. Holland was the Chief of the 92d Bombardment Wing Standardization and Evaluation Section at Fairchild Air Force Base. *This position made him responsible for the knowledge and enforcement of academic and in-flight standards for the wing's flying operations.* He was regarded by many as an outstanding pilot, perhaps the best in the entire B-52 fleet. He was an experienced instructor pilot and had served with the Strategic Air Command's 1st Combat Evaluation Group (CEVG), considered by many aviators to be the "top of the pyramid." Selecting an aviator who exercised poor airmanship as the Chief of Standard and Evaluation's was a poor choice, but leaving him there after multiple flagrant and willful violations of regulations sent an extremely negative message to the rest of the wing flyers.

Individuals who hold key positions are looked up to as role models by junior crew members. They must be removed if they cannot maintain an acceptable standard of professionalism. Even if Holland had not crashed, the damage he had done through his bad example of airmanship is incalculable. Not only did many young officers see his lack of professionalism as a bad example, but they also observed several senior leaders witness his actions and fail to take any corrective action.

Prior to the accident, Holland and the rest of his flight crew, who were professionally at odds, were to be paired in the cockpit for the next several months. One of the crew members had confided in his wife that he did not trust Holland to fly with his aircrews.

What is not mentioned in any of these accounts is the "culture" that allowed this pilot to continue to fly, despite the evidence he was unsafe. In medicine, as physicians, we are often in charge of "policing" ourselves when we see poor, inadequate, negligent care of a patient. But how often do we actually intervene if we are a trainee or subordinate?

Medical culture is remarkably similar to military culture, which is why I want to point out the sequence of events that led to this tragedy. In medicine, as in the military, there is a "chain of command." For example, the attending is responsible for the fellows, chief residents, junior residents, interns and finally, medical students.

There is a clear distinction between each trainee and the level of responsibility for each position. What do trainees who see a superior engage in willful misconduct or behavior do? It is an exceedingly difficult situation for the observer, not the one who is engaged in the behavior. It's exceptionally challenging if the individual is at the top of the chain of command and in charge of safety, as Holland was.

The Fairchild accident is unique in that Holland's superiors never intervened effectively. The junior pilots and officers could have and should have had the ability to express their collective concerns to someone in a position of authority above Holland without fear of reprimand, but that's the rub. I am certain there was fear of reprimand from reporting a pilot who has a reputation of being "the best." Even "the best" pilots and physicians make errors from time to time. But Holland repeatedly violated safety and protocol, and there is a big difference between an occasional mistake and a repeated pattern.

For problem physicians who engage in repeated behaviors, you create hard lines in the sand they can no longer cross, and if they do, they lose their privileges. Corrective action is not an option because patient safety trumps everything.

Holland's commanding officers had a responsibility to report and document the discussions, and after the second incident, he should have been grounded. Yet, the "discussions" were not documented or there was no action taken. We have a responsibility to first create and maintain a safe environment for the care our patients receive, and there should never be a compromise due to a complacent culture.

At the conclusion of the investigation, the U.S. Air Force circulated the findings of this accident throughout the rest of the service as a reminder of the importance of adhering to safety regulations and maintaining an open "chain of command" responsible for enforcing and disciplining those who choose to ignore them.

There is nothing more toxic and corrosive than a disruptive physician leader. A lazy or dishonest department chair, Chief of Staff, or CMO can quickly derail an organization and create chaos and dysfunction. I have seen physician leaders derail medical staff meetings through inappropriate comments, political jabs, relentless complaining, and open hostility. Approaching and managing a disruptive physician leader is a difficult, politically charged situation with a lot of downside risk for nearly all parties.

The silver lining, if there is any, is that the same techniques learned from managing other behaviors have utility in these situations as well. If a department chair is not completing peer reviews, investigating professional behavior complaints, or regularly attending department chair meetings, the first task is to find out why. When I was Chief of Staff, one of the department chairs showed up only once or twice per year to our Medical Executive Committee meetings, and when this individual did attend, it was only to provide input or create discussion on topics relevant to the department he was representing. At one meeting, other department chairs pointed out to him his absence unless he had an agenda. The department chair had no defense, and those who spoke up did so professionally and directly. It was good medicine. He started attending meetings more regularly.

Some physician leaders do not model the professional behaviors of their leadership role. A service line chair regularly showed up 30 minutes after his OR start-time. Another chair regularly criticized hospital administration in the doctor's lounge. And yet another used his position as chair to advance his group's business goals and strategic plans. In some of these cases, it is exceptionally difficult to intervene without creating a lot of political chaos.

If conflicts of interest can be proven, the medical executive committee has a duty to intervene to preserve the integrity of the committee. The context of the conflict should determine precisely how it is managed, but generally, where a medical staff member's interest conflicts with the medical staff's interests, the member must stand down and remove themself from the decision being made. Thus, if the conflict affects a pending decision, the member should recuse themself from voting in that instance.

If the member fails or refuses to do so, the leader of the meeting should excuse the member from the vote. Members of the affected committee or department should be empowered to vote a member out of the meeting if recusal or excuse does not occur. The committee or leader may force the member out of the vote or may bar the conflicted member from participating in the discussion entirely. Developing a conflict disclosure form that reflects the relevant bylaw provisions can help both members and leaders understand and implement conflict of interest procedures in medical staff meetings and elections.

In some instances, too, the Chief Medical Officer or Chief of Staff may recommend the removal of chairs who are not fulfilling their responsibilities. Those responsibilities are usually outlined in detail in the medical staff bylaws. The best approach is to suggest the individual resign from the position. If not, and the behavior is egregious enough, most bylaws contain proceedings for removing chairs from the position. This should be your last resort.

A key aspect of physician leadership is that there is *always* an individual, usually a superior or a board of directors, who has the authority to intervene. If it is the CEO, the BOD can intervene. If it is a member of the BOD, the chair of the BOD can intervene. If it is the CMO, the CEO can intervene. Every medical staff leader has a duty and responsibility to act in the organization's best interests and to fulfill their responsibilities as outlined in the bylaws.

REFERENCES

1. Spencer L, Barnett JT. When Men Are Sexually Harassed: A Foundation for Studying Men's Experiences as Targets of Sexual Harassment. *Speaker & Gael.* 2011;48(2):53–67.

2. Carr P, Ash A, Friedman R. Faculty Perceptions of Gender Discrimination and Sexual Harassment in Academic Medicine. *Annals of Internal Medicine.* 2000;132(1): 889–896.

3. Back C, Freeman W. Sexual Harassment and Title VII: Selected Legal Issues. *Congressional Research Service.* April 9, 2018.

4. U.S. Equal Employment Opportunity Commission. Sexual Harassment. Retrieved from: www.eeoc.gov/sexual-harassment.

5. Rihal CS, Baker NA, Bunkers BE, et al. Addressing Sexual Harassment in the #MeToo Era: An Institutional Approach. *Mayo Clinic Proceedings.* 2020;95(4):749–757.

6. . Fisher D. Former Claremont Doctor Pleads Guilty to Assaulting Patient, Could Practice Medicine Again. *Union Leader.* March 23, 2021.

7. Garman J. Accusations of Sexual Misconduct or Harassment Against Physicians. Medical Board of California. www.mbc.ca.gov/Licensing/Physicians-and-Surgeons/ Practice-Information/Sexual-Misconduct.aspx

8. Petrozzello D. How To Handle Romantic Advances from a Patient. *ENT Today.* August 1, 2013.

9. Gulrajani C. A Duty To Protect Our Patients From Physician Sexual Misconduct. *The Journal of the American Academy of Psychiatry and the Law.* 2020 June;48(2): 176–180. DOI: https://doi.org/10.29158/JAAPL.200014-20

10. Becker's Hospital Review. Police: Ohio Physician Arrested, Charged with Assault Following Dispute with Colleague. April 28, 2021.

11. Volz N, Fringer R, Walters B, Kowalenko T. Prevalence of Horizontal Violence Among Emergency Attending Physicians, Residents, and Physician Assistants. *Western Journal of Emergency Medicine*. 2017;18(2):213–218.

12. Rainford W, Wood S, McMullen P, Phipsen N. The Disruptive Force of Lateral Violence in the Health Care Setting. Continuing Education Module. *The Journal for Nurse Practitioners*. 2015;11(2):157–164.

13. Bambi S, Guazzini A, De Felippis C, Lucchini A, Rasero, L. Preventing Workplace Incivility, Lateral Violence and Bullying Between Nurses. A Narrative Literature Review. 2017;88,(Suppl5): 39–47.

14. Warner DO, Berge K, Sun H, et al. Substance Use Disorder in Physicians after Completion of Training in Anesthesiology in the United States from 1977 to 2013. *Anesthesiology*. 2020:133:342–349.

15. Joos L, Glazemakers I, and Dom G. Alcohol Use and Hazardous Drinking Among Medical Specialists. *European Addiction Research*. 2013;19(2):89–97.

16. Kern T. *Darker Shades of Blue: A Case Study of Failed Leadership*. 1995. https://convergentperformance.com/wp-content/uploads/attachments/Darker_Shades_of_Blue.pdf.

CHAPTER 8

Avoiding Pitfalls:
The Legal Minefield

"A law is valuable, not because it is a law,
but because there is right in it."

– Henry Ward Beecher

As a leader, you have a responsibility to document your communications and actions in both peer review and physician conduct. In the following chapters, I discuss fair hearings, legal counsel's role, human resource's role, and the rapid changes in the process as physicians are now employed in large physician groups or hospitals and hospital systems.

DUE PROCESS AND FAIR HEARINGS

Physician leaders must adhere strictly to policy and due process. The due process clause of the 14th Amendment of the U.S. Constitution states, " . . . nor shall any State deprive any person of life, liberty, or property, without due process of law . . ." When the government takes action to deprive an individual of a right, a hearing takes place prior to the deprivation of that right when the contested right involves "property interests" of the individual.

In the medical setting, when depriving a physician of a right to practice medicine through terminating privileges or suspending a medical license, the physician is entitled to a hearing. In *Darlak v. Bobear* (5th Cir. 1987), the court determined that an informal hearing satisfied the due process rights of a temporarily suspended physician. In summary, the courts have determined that medical staff privileges are a "property interest."

The Health Care Quality Improvement Act of 1986 (HCQIA) was passed to provide qualified immunity for peer review committee members and to specify physicians' rights at a fair hearing. The rights of a physician include at least a 30-day notice prior to a hearing. Also included are the right to a mutually acceptable hearing officer, the right to legal representation, the right to a record of the hearing, the right to call and examine witnesses, the right to present evidence, the right to submit a written statement at the conclusion of the hearing, and finally, the right to receive written communication of the decision and appeal.

Importantly, hospitals conducting fair hearing procedures, and the physicians on the peer review or Professional Behavior Committee, are immune from liability under the HCQIA. However, only good faith peer review qualifies for HCQIA protection. Good faith peer review means it is objective, transparent, free from conflicts of interest, and follows due process.

Prior to the HCQIA, the physician members of the committees terminating a physician's privileges could be sued. Since passage of the HCQIA, the intent of the law to protect members who conduct good faith peer review was upheld in *Mathews vs Lancaster General Hospital* (Pa, 1996). Of note, the HCQIA does not include advanced practice providers such as physician assistants, nurse practitioners, or other allied health professionals who are not physicians or dentists. With increasing numbers of allied health professionals providing care in hospital settings, including these practitioners in this process will need to be incorporated into the bylaws of most organizations.

Failure to follow due process remains the primary reason physicians file an appeal to a hearing result.[1] The second and third reasons are breach of contract and bad faith, malice, and conspiracy. In *Sherr v Healtheast Care System* a neurosurgeon with privileges at two hospitals filed a lawsuit after a competing inhouse neurosurgical group sought his ouster by, according to him, defaming his medical skills and arranging sham peer review processes.[2] The result was a summary suspension of his privileges. The competing group labeled the physician as a "hack, not a good surgeon, and an asshole."

The peer-review process was strictly adhered to, and the physician did not win the appeal, as his outcomes were not meeting the standard of care. It is interesting to note the language used to describe the surgeon in this case. Although professional conduct is not mentioned, it is highly likely the physician had strained and poor relationships with many of the staff. It is not uncommon for a physician who has multiple conduct concerns to also have an increased number of complications or poor outcomes. I have no evidence and cannot cite a study confirming this statement, but I suspect a formal study would find a strong correlation.

LEGAL COUNSEL'S ROLE AND WHEN TO SEEK COUNSEL

Most large physician groups and hospitals have employed attorneys who can assist physician leaders as they process a behavior complaint. It is not always necessary to involve legal counsel, but if the behavior is egregious enough or the physician has a long-standing history of professional behavior complaints without resolution, it is in their best interest to discuss proceedings with counsel regardless of disposition.

An experienced attorney who has handled medical staff affairs issues and cases is a valuable asset. In my own experience, without legal counsel's guidance, I would have made procedural or documentation errors in some of the cases I described earlier.

It is especially important to discuss matters with legal counsel if you or the committee decide to terminate or limit the privileges of a physician. Mandating that a physician take a professionalism course or complete focused continuing education is reasonable. If the physician fails to complete the courses, and consequences are clearly communicated, including termination of privileges, confidence in this as the correct course of action is supported through consulting counsel. Attorneys can ensure you are following due process. Avoid the landmines if possible.

HUMAN RESOURCE'S MANAGEMENT AND ROLE

Twenty years ago, human resources departments were rarely involved directly with physicians and professional conduct, as most physicians were part of large, independent practice groups or solo practitioners with privileges. As of 2019, most of the physician workforce is now employed.[3] Human resource departments now bear some responsibility in both hiring and terminating physicians from hospitals and large national group practices.

Unfortunately, this situation presents potential issues regarding the legal process, rights of the physician, etc. Whether employed or not, most professional behavior processes are handled within the governance and leadership structure set for in the bylaws for the medical staff. This is reflective of the traditional process, and most organizations continue to utilize a Medical Executive Committee or a similar committee established by the bylaws.

As employees, most physicians have contracts that include sections on separation or termination. To protect the employer, termination both with and without cause is an option. A "without cause" termination in physician employment contracts allows the physician or the employer to terminate employment even though the other party has done nothing wrong. "Without cause" termination provisions are a dual-edged sword. They give the physician the right to leave for no reason, but they also give the employer the right to give the physician the boot for no reason.

Only two major aspects of this provision require the attention of the physician: the amount of notice and assurance that both parties have the same notice period.[4]

"With cause" termination is self-explanatory. Most physician contracts include professional conduct examples. In the case example of the ICU physician who verbally abused nurses, his employer terminated him. The MEC did not need to get involved, as this was an internal human resource department concern with the parent company.

If the physician is employed by a large national group and the group has a contract with the hospital or hospital system, the contracts between the hospital and the group can give the hospital the right to terminate a contracted physician. I saw this take place at two institutions in the past year. In both cases, the decisions were justified.

The upside as a physician leader in handling conduct concerns or the decision to terminate an employed physician is that the process is usually quicker and easier. Going through the MEC and the fair hearing process takes months, and with appeals, it may take even more time. The politics, time, and resources involved in going this route can be exhausting for everyone. The downside as a physician is that the inherent protection afforded the MEC route no longer applies.

Remember that the hospital has a responsibility to preserve and maintain a non-hostile work environment for its employees. Whether the physician is employed or not, if the physician continues to create a hostile work environment and the MEC or hospital or physician's employer fails to take corrective actions, employees can sue. It is most common for employees to sue for sexual harassment. Hospitals and physicians have lost cases when they have fired nurses who file complaints or grievances about bullying and harassment. Hospitals have a duty to document reports of misconduct. In 2016, a nurse was awarded $440,000 after reporting an incident and then subsequently being fired as a result of the report.[5]

Dr. Marty Martin and Dr. Philip Hemphill suggest human resource departments train staff members on managing disruptive behaviors and create a designated position to examine policies and procedures related to disruptive behaviors. Having someone with expertise on these matters in human resources can be a great asset and help you avoid pitfalls. Lastly, and I mention this in the Board of Directors' role, someone should regularly report the number of conduct complaints and how the organization is reducing or mitigating the complaints.[6]

STATE MEDICAL BOARDS AND THE NATIONAL PRACTITIONER DATABANK

All state medical boards have policies and procedures, and the legal authority, to revoke a physician's medical license if the physician is found to be unfit for duty secondary to substance use disorder, medical conditions, egregious professional behavior, or clinical concerns. Board action is the result of longstanding concerns or one singular event. Hospital leaders are legally obligated to report to their respective state medical boards any actions against a physician limiting or revoking privileges. Here is an example from the Iowa Board of Medicine:

> *A full and confidential report concerning any final hospital disciplinary action approved by a hospital board of trustees that results in a limitation, suspension, or revocation of a physician's privilege to practice for reasons relating to the physician's professional competence or professional conduct, or concerning any voluntary surrender or limitation of privileges for reasons relating to professional competence or professional conduct shall be made to the board by the hospital administrator or chief of medical staff within ten days of such action.*

Additionally, if a physician has lost privileges at a hospital and the appropriate medical board is notified, the physician must then disclose this action to all other state medical boards where the physician has a license:

> *Each licensee, including a licensee holding an inactive license, shall report to the board every license revocation, suspension or other disciplinary action taken against the licensee by a professional licensing authority of another state, an agency of the United States government, or any country, territory, or other jurisdiction. The report must be filed with the board within 30 days from the date of the action against the physician's license.*

To avoid disciplinary action, some physicians have voluntarily resigned their privileges while under investigation. In the past, this strategy worked, but most medical boards will be notified if a physician is under investigation, so it's best to be honest.

Recently, I learned of a physician who left one state to practice in another state after the physician's former state of practice had completed an investigation, determined disposition, and put forth a course of action for mishandling controlled drugs. The physician was required to pay a small fine and complete focused CME courses. According to secondhand sources, the physician never disclosed any of this information to the new employer, including the prior medical board's actions. The current employer discovered the other state medical board suspended the physician's license to practice, as the requirements were not completed. Due to failure to honestly disclose any of these events, the physician was immediately terminated. This is unfortunate, but clearly, the physician's lack of honesty and failure to complete the requirements was a justified reason to terminate.

A large gap, and failure, in my opinion, is the lack of a rapid system to communicate these actions openly with other state medical boards. Though this physician's actions in no way caused patient harm, this is both an individual and *system* failure.

HOSPITAL ADMINISTRATION'S ROLE

CEO's Role

The CEO is the public "face" of the hospital. Though not solely responsible for physician conduct, if a physician engages in misconduct and it remains unresolved or becomes "headline news," the CEO must answer the hard questions in front of a media hungry for all of the sordid details. In some cases of sexual misconduct found to have been "covered up," the CEO is often held accountable for the lapses in addressing the misconduct. CEOs have a responsibility to know about "problem" physicians.

Regular check-ins with the other C-suite executives, specifically the CMO, Chief of Staff, or Vice-President of Medical Affairs, can keep CEOs informed of potential problem physicians. There is nothing worse than for a CEO to be blindsided by a conduct complaint, or worse, multiple conduct complaints. Building relationships with senior physician leaders is critical in helping manage problem physicians. It is reasonable for the CEO to expect the CMO or whoever is responsible for managing disruptive behavior to hold themselves and others accountable.

CEOs also have a responsibility to remain largely impartial and objective and not have "favorites." Imagine this scenario: The CEO of a large urban hospital is friends with a surgeon who generates millions of dollars in revenue. The two are often seen golfing on weekends, and the families regularly get together for social events. The physician is accused of pushing a nurse out of the way in the OR who, unfortunately, fell and hit her head on a surgical table, splitting it open. There are three witnesses to the event who state it was obvious the physician pushed the nurse during an angry outburst.

The nurse is now threatening assault charges against the physician, stating that he intentionally pushed her out of the way and has a habit of mistreating staff. You are the new CMO and responsible for investigating this incident. The CEO invites you into his office for a meeting about the incident, as he was made aware of it immediately by the Chief Nursing Officer. It was nearly impossible to contain the details of the incident, as the OR staff knew what had occurred and the news spread fast.

Despite the CEO's friendship with the attributed physician, there must be objective, impartial treatment of the physician, and as the CMO, you need to communicate this with the CEO. These are difficult conversations, but any attempt to influence the outcome of an investigation favoring the physician because of the friendship or financial impact on the hospital is unethical.

Chief Medical Officer's Role

The role of the Chief Medical Officer (CMO) has changed dramatically in the past two decades. Increasingly, CMOs are participating in business strategy, ensuring quality outcomes, and managing physician conduct.

The job requirements have also changed considerably, with many CMOs now required to obtain MBAs, MHAs, MMM, or certification as physician executives through the American Association of Physician Leadership (AAPL) or fellowship with the American College of Healthcare Executives (FACHE). As true C-suite leaders, the CMO, CFO, CEO, and CNO often work in tandem.

CMOs are an integral liaison between the C-suite and other physician leaders in the organization. As a result, many healthcare organizations rely on CMOs to manage the professional behavior of the medical staff. This has several advantages compared to using department chairs or the president of the medical staff. First, the CMO often does not have a professional working relationship with attributed physicians. This reduces the potential for conflicts of interest and helps preserve the objectivity of any investigation or disposition. An additional advantage is the CMO is aware of the broader issues in the organization. If professional behavior is a widespread problem, then a systemic effort will help reduce the problem. Department chairs often lack this perspective, and it is outside their scope and role beyond their own departments.

In other systems, the CMO is tasked with training or mentoring chairs on managing quality and/or professional conduct. In large healthcare systems, a CMO may not have adequate time or resources to investigate all concerns, and the CMO may only be asked to intervene directly for egregious conduct. In my experience, having an experienced CMO involved in managing professional conduct is advantageous for the organization and other medical staff leaders.

Medical Executive Committee's Role

Medical executive committees (MECs) are composed of senior leaders of the medical staff who are responsible for approving policies, credentialing physicians, ensuring quality, and in some cases, overseeing professional behaviors. Interestingly, MECs are a relatively new organizational construct for the medical staff. The Joint Commission mandated the creation of the MEC in 1980 as a newer model to provide staff governance. Prior to this, medical staffs were loosely organized, and decisions were made by a majority vote during monthly or annual all-staff meetings. The MEC transformed the medical staff from democracy to a representative republic.

An important development is the requirement for MECs to move from autonomy to accountability.[7] Being accountable means reducing and mitigating professional behavior conduct proactively and objectively.

Board of Directors' Role

The hospital board of directors (BOD) is ultimately accountable and responsible for the delivery of healthcare for the institution. Although not involved in daily operations and management, the BOD is charged with ensuring the environment for the provision of care meets regulatory and compliance requirements. An additional responsibility is ensuring the organization is making efforts to provide quality care in a safe, supportive work environment.

If quality care is compromised secondary to the tolerance or mismanagement of disruptive physician behaviors, the board of directors is responsible — whether or not there is direct knowledge of the behavioral impact. A continuing problem with many hospital BODs is a lack of formal education and training for members around BOD responsibilities. The University of North Dakota Center for Rural Health published a brief document on the Board's Role in Quality, and it states:

Board members are legally responsible for the quality of the health care delivered within their organizations. The board is accountable for the actions or lack of actions of every person within the organization, including the medical staff. The board is responsible for ensuring effective systems exist for evaluating and improving the delivery of high-quality care.[8]

Most hospital board members receive little training or understand their role and responsibilities as a member of the BOD. In rural hospitals, even fewer BOD members receive training. Most BOD members do not routinely receive dashboards on the prevalence of professional behavior complaints. With anonymous reporting systems, it is easy to create a dashboard and set goals for the reduction of complaints. If it cannot be measured, it cannot be improved.

REFERENCES

1. Rosenstein A, Karwaki T, King K. Legal Entanglements in Dealing with Disruptive Behavior. *Physician Leadership Journal.* May/June 2016: 46–51.

2. Hodge S. What Can be Done About a Disruptive Physician? A Legal Analysis. *Pace Law Review.* 2020;40(1):126–153.

3. Bannow T. Nearly 70% of U. S. Physicians Now Employed by Hospitals or Corporations, Report Finds. *Modern Healthcare.* June 29, 2021. Retrieved from www.modernhealthcare.com/providers/nearly-70-us-physicians-now-employed-hospitals-or-corporations-report-finds

4. Hursh D. Without Cause Termination in Physician Contracts. Physician Agreements Health Law. 2015. *Retrieved from:* https://pahealthlaw.com/without-cause-termination-in-physician-employment-contracts/.

5. Downs C. Grapevine Clinic to Pay Fired Nurse $440k in Discrimination, Bullying Lawsuit. *The Dallas Morning News.* August 9, 2016.

6. Martin W, Hemphill P. *Taming Disruptive Behavior.* Tampa, FL: AAPL; 2012.

7. Burroughs J. *Redesign the Medical Staff Model: A Guide to Collaborative Change.* Chicago, IL: Health Administration Press; 2015.

8. The Board's Role. Health Care Boards in the 21st Century. D.D. Bainbridge & Associates, Inc; 2006.

CHAPTER 9

Personality Types and Personality Disorders: Behavioral Impact and Management

Personality has power to uplift, power to depress,
power to curse, and power to bless.

– Paul P. Harris

MOST PHYSICIANS ARE HARD-WORKING, DRIVEN, compassionate, intelligent individuals who strive to provide excellent patient care. The *individual* achievement and skills required to get into medical school and complete residency are not necessarily translatable as the physician becomes a partner or employee in a large group practice after training.

Increasingly, physicians are care team leaders tasked with supervising and managing groups of physician extenders and nurse practitioners in a complex healthcare setting. It is an environment ripe for interpersonal conflicts and negative behaviors from all parties — not just the physicians.

This new model is a radical change from practice just three or four decades ago when a solo physician could literally hang a shingle and practice or was expected to round, personally on all his or her patients. Most physicians have adapted to these recent changes and new expectations, but some have not. These physicians who struggle lament the loss of autonomy and what might be perceived as a challenge to their authority with the presence of other team members.

Personality profoundly affects an individual's perception and response to their environment, and a working definition of personality is necessary while discussing the traits, profiles, and Axis II disorders that influence

111

personal behavior. Recent, validated research has identified five distinct domains of personality[1]:

1. **Agreeableness** is a measure of an individual's tendencies with respect to social harmony. This trait reflects how well the individual gets along with others, how cooperative or skeptical they are, and how they might interact within a team.

2. **Conscientiousness** is a measure of how careful, deliberate, self-disciplined, and organized an individual is. Conscientiousness is often predictive of employee productivity.

3. **Extraversion** is a measure of how sociable, outgoing, and energetic an individual is. Individuals who score lower on the extraversion scale are more introverted, or more deliberate, quiet, low-key, and independent.

4. **Openness** measures the extent to which an individual is imaginative and creative, as opposed to down-to-earth and conventional.

5. **Stress Tolerance** measures the ways in which individuals react to stress.

The scientifically validated Big Five Test is widely used in academia to measure these five domains. A more popular and well-known personality test is the Myers-Briggs Personality Test, which identifies 16 distinct personality types. Despite the popularity and widespread use of the Myers-Briggs Personality Test, the results have been the subject of continued controversy for decades, and this limits its utility.

Regardless of the tool used to measure personality, it is important to note that personality traits are mutable over time. As a physician leader, recognizing these distinct personalities and their influences on behavior helps provide a customized road map for communication and interaction with the physician. A one-size-fits all approach is a pitfall, and what is effective with one physician may not be the best approach for another physician.

PERSONALITY TRAITS AND PROFILES OF DISRUPTIVE PHYSICIANS

A physician's personality influences their career and certainly impacts their practice environment. Hicks and McCracken delineate the traits and domains into three categories that are useful for physician leaders to understand: interpersonal traits, self-control traits, and personal contentment with their career.[2] It is important to note that traits are distinctly different from personality disorders, which will be discussed in greater detail later in this chapter.

Physicians with interpersonal traits described as anti-social in nature are often "loners." They exhibit low sociability and lack trust in others. These physicians, when they do attend department or medical staff meetings, are quiet and rarely speak up in front of the group. However, after the meeting, they might subvert and sabotage the committee's or another physician's efforts to create change through passive-aggressive maneuvers, including having private, undocumented conversations with hidden agendas intended to benefit the physician at the expense of the organization or other colleagues.

These physicians want to remain in control, and any loss of control is a threat — leading to the potential for disruptive behavior. They often are not part of larger group practices. They simply do not fit into any type of work culture due to their anti-social traits. Fortunately, physicians who exhibit these traits are rare.

The literature on emotional intelligence and long-term professional success reveals that individuals with great emotional self-control are unlikely to be disruptive.[2] Physicians with a high degree of emotional intelligence and sociability are keenly aware of how others perceive them, and they know how to navigate the personal-political environment. These physicians are good leaders. Most department chairs, CMO, and other leadership positions are occupied by physicians with a great deal of emotional control and awareness. Physicians with low self-control are prone to react to stressful situations with dramatic responses — leading to a variety of disruptive behaviors that can derail their careers.

Getting these physicians to change their behavior and control their emotions is not an easy task. In some extreme cases, professional counseling and anger management workshops are necessary. This drives home one of the major points of this book: The goal is positive change and rehabilitation, not punishment. The physician deserves a chance to correct the behavior, but if the behavior continues, it must be made clear the physician is at risk of losing privileges or, if employed, termination.

Personal contentment is, perhaps, the most difficult trait to assess and change. In fact, it is more accurate to state that personal contentment is a mood more than a traditional trait. Most physicians know partners or colleagues who are consistently negative or seem unhappy. They do not necessarily like the practice of medicine or circumstances and never really see the big picture and are not optimistic about the future.[3] For some of these physicians, there can be undiagnosed and untreated mood disorders. If there is an untreated mood disorder, gently suggesting professional intervention with a psychiatrist or psychologist is helpful if the physician seems open to the suggestion. These physicians are not necessarily "disruptive" in the traditional sense, but their mood can keep a practice from thriving.

Roback, et al. examined personality profiles of physicians by the type of behavioral complaint.[4] As early as 1981, Dorr recognized the literature on disruptive physicians is rich with "clinical observations," but there was a paucity of quantitative data.[5]

Eight-eight physicians referred to the Vanderbilt Comprehensive Assessment Program completed the Minnesota Multiphasic Personality-2 (MMPI-2) and the Personality Assessment Inventory (PAI). Behavior types were categorized into three types: sexual boundary violators, behaviorally disruptive, or "other" misconduct. This was the first study to examine personality type and category of offense. Not surprisingly, the physicians who were referred to the program due to sexual boundary violations had the fewest normal profiles and produced the highest percentage of MMPI-2 and PAI profiles indicating character disorder.[4] This group exhibited little self-control, high impulsivity, less empathy, and were least likely to accept responsibility. This is consistent with Abel and Osborn's clinical finding that "physicians involved in sexual misconduct usually show minimal appreciation of the plight of their victims."[6]

The "behaviorally disruptive" physicians' personality profiles reveal key differences from the sexual boundary group. Behaviorally disruptive physicians are more open to the process and have a "greater willingness to admit to personal shortcomings."[4] Of note, the physicians in the study freely admitted to angry outbursts, but several of them justified the response. For example, some physicians rationalize the angry outbursts as a display of their "passion to heal." This passion, combined with little or no self-control, leads to abusive language, yelling, and disparaging remarks. Ultimately, these behaviors can lead to the end of a physician's career if the behavior is egregious enough.

Changing physician personality is not possible; it is hard-wired. However, changing a physician's self-awareness and offering constructive internal tools to help manage emotions and behavior is possible. Rehabilitation is possible for many of these physicians if the process for addressing it is constructive and the physician is offered timely, consistent, supportive feedback.

PERSONALITY DISORDERS AND THE DISRUPTIVE PHYSICIAN

Physicians with personality disorders, also referred to as Axis II disorders, are difficult to diagnose and manage. Fortunately, the prevalence in the general population is less than 4% and in physicians, is roughly 2%.[7] There are three distinct Axis II disorder cluster types (see Figure 1).

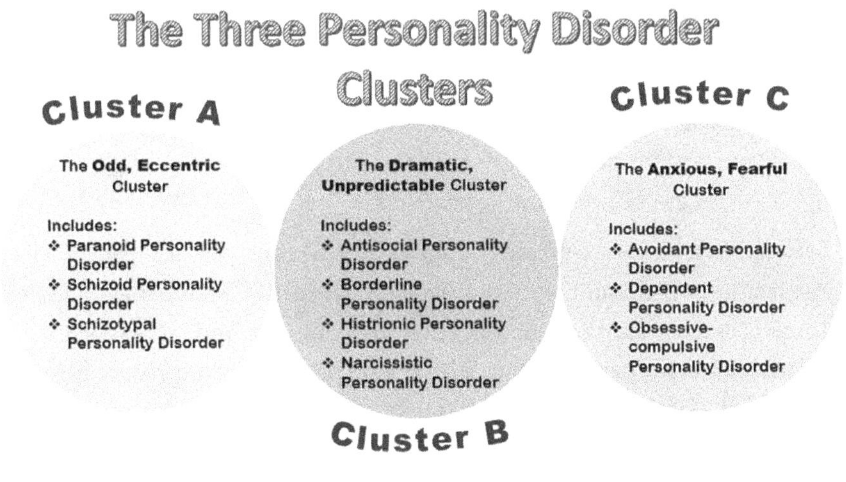

The Three Personality Disorder Clusters

Cluster A

The **Odd, Eccentric** Cluster

Includes:
❖ Paranoid Personality Disorder
❖ Schizoid Personality Disorder
❖ Schizotypal Personality Disorder

Cluster B

The **Dramatic, Unpredictable** Cluster

Includes:
❖ Antisocial Personality Disorder
❖ Borderline Personality Disorder
❖ Histrionic Personality Disorder
❖ Narcissistic Personality Disorder

Cluster C

The **Anxious, Fearful** Cluster

Includes:
❖ Avoidant Personality Disorder
❖ Dependent Personality Disorder
❖ Obsessive-compulsive Personality Disorder

FIGURE 1. The Three Personality Disorder Clusters

The prevalence of personality disorders is lower in physicians than the general population due to self-selection out of a career in medicine. This makes intuitive sense. Despite the low prevalence, physicians with personality disorders are most commonly cluster type B or C. Of those in cluster B, anti-social and narcissistic personality disorders are most common. Among those physicians in cluster C, obsessive-compulsive and avoidant personality disorders are most common.

As a physician leader, the only way you can identify whether a physician is suffering from one of these personality disorders is to observe behaviors. These conditions are distinct from mood disorders, and this is critical. If a physician is making no progress with continued interventions after multiple disruptive episodes, despite escalating consequences, you should consider whether the physician does indeed suffer from a personality disorder.

Earlier in the chapter, I briefly described the anti-social personality. The following is a more comprehensive list of behaviors and traits of anti-social personality disorder:

- Frequent, angry outbursts
- Arrogance
- Manipulating others
- Acting witty and charming for personal gain
- Frequent lying
- Stealing
- Verbally aggressive
- Frequent, physical altercations
- Breaking institutional rules and norms
- Disregard for personal safety or the safety of others
- Lack of guilt or remorse for actions

These physicians are prone to angry outbursts and physical threats, defy organizational rules, and often lack insight or empathy. Their behavior lowers morale, creates a harmful and negative environment, and increases organizational liability. As a leader, you have a responsibility to protect hospital staff and the organization. An effective approach is to set boundaries for the behaviors and escalate consequences using the organization's code of conduct and bylaws.

Your authority is a threat to these physicians, and you must make it clear to them that their behavior will not be tolerated. As discussed in other chapters, it is essential to document complaints and meetings and always have a witness or witnesses present during any discussion. These physicians often retain counsel and use the legal system to their advantage. Ensure you and the organization have followed the process as stated in the bylaws and document everything.

I cannot emphasize enough the importance of accurate, timely documentation. It is critical if the organization is considering terminating an employed physician. If the hospital has a contract with a separate group, the only recourse is revoking privileges. If the hospital is considering revoking privileges, which is a reportable event for most state medical boards, ensure that you are following due process.

Narcissistic personality disorder is not common in the general population (less than 0.5%), but it is more prevalent in physicians. As many as one in five medical students has narcissistic traits,[8] which include:

- Having an exaggerated sense of self-importance.
- Having a sense of entitlement and require constant, excessive admiration.
- Expecting recognition as superior even without achievements that warrant it.
- Exaggerating achievements and talents.
- Being preoccupied with fantasies about success, power, brilliance, beauty, or the perfect mate.
- Believing they are superior and can only associate with equally special people.
- Monopolizing conversations and belittling or looking down on people they perceive as inferior.
- Expecting special favors and unquestioning compliance with their expectations.
- Taking advantage of others to get what they want.
- Being unable or unwilling to recognize the needs and feelings of others.
- Being envious of others and believing others envy them.
- Behaving in an arrogant or haughty manner, coming across as conceited, boastful, and pretentious.
- Insisting on having the best of everything — for instance, the best car or office.

At the same time, people with narcissistic personality disorder have trouble handling anything they perceive as criticism, and they can:

- Become impatient or angry when they do not receive special treatment.
- Have significant interpersonal problems and easily feel slighted.
- React with rage or contempt and try to belittle the other person to make themselves appear superior.
- Have difficulty regulating emotions and behavior.
- Experience major problems dealing with stress and adapting to change.

- Feel depressed and moody because they fall short of perfection.
- Have secret feelings of insecurity, shame, vulnerability, and humiliation.

These physicians can hijack a department or meeting and take complete control. Since they feel such a high degree of entitlement, they can sabotage a team or project and create a lot of chaos. Like the anti-social personality, the individual with narcissism believes the world revolves around them and their needs and goals; their ego runs their world.

The common trait shared by people with either narcissistic or anti-social personality disorder is a lack of empathy and compassion. Fortunately, these physicians often do not engage in verbal or threatening behaviors. However, they can and often do engage in more insidious behaviors, including constantly threatening to leave the organization, insisting their needs are more important than another physician's or the organization's needs, and belittling colleagues.

A key strategy in managing these physicians is clear boundary setting. As a physician leader, you must clearly communicate that the behaviors that create a chaotic environment will not be tolerated.

Physicians with Cluster C personality disorders are not very disruptive. This is especially true for those with an avoidant personality disorder. They share similar traits with Cluster B personality disorders, but these physicians rarely create a chaotic environment. Those with avoidant personality disorder:

- Are easily hurt when people criticize or disapprove of them.
- Hold back too much in intimate relationships.
- Are reluctant to become involved with people.
- Avoid activities or jobs that involve contact with others.
- Are shy in social situations out of fear of doing something wrong.
- Make potential difficulties seem worse than they are.
- Hold the view they are not good socially, not as good as other people, or unappealing.

Physicians with avoidant personality disorders are exceptionally rare. Their "disruptive" behavior often is a total lack of engagement with others. Afraid of social contact, they may intentionally avoid phone calls, meetings, etc. These behaviors can undermine the workflow and day-to-day operations of a clinic or lab.

Another approach is to categorize a physician by archetype. Broadly, physicians can be lumped into one of four categories: the know-it-all, the flake, the insecure, and the combatant. The know-it-all physician can be condescending, unapproachable, and intimidating. Narcissistic traits are evident in a know-it-all physician. Insecure physicians doubt their ability, seek affirmation, and can be indecisive. Of the four types, these physicians are not disruptive in the traditional sense other than their lack of confidence can lead to nurses and colleagues not trusting their abilities.

The flake physician is the physician who does not respond to calls, fails to complete charts, and may be chronically late to meetings or clinics. Lastly, the combatant physician is exactly as described: confrontational, accusatory, emotionally labile, and prone to bullying behavior.

Take time to reflect on the specific behaviors and attitudes of the physician within the context of their personality type. Your communication style with the physician based on your understanding of his or her personality can influence and impact your effectiveness and the outcome.

REFERENCES

1. Widiger T, Crego C. The Five Factor Model of Personality Structure: An Update. *World Psychiatry*. 2019;18(3):271–272.
2. Hicks R, McCracken J. Personality Traits of a Disruptive Physician. *Physician Executive Journal*. 2012;38(5): 66–68.
3. Brackett M, Rivers, S, Salovey, P. Emotional Intelligence: Implications for Personal, Social, Academic, and Workplace Success. *Social and Personality Compass*. 2012;5(1): 88–103.
4. Roback H, Strassberg D, Iannelli R., et al. Problematic Physicians: A Comparison of Personality Profiles by Offense Type. *The Canadian Journal of Psychiatry*. 2007:52(5): 315–322.
5. Dorr D. MMPI Profiles of Emotionally Impaired Physicians. *Journal of Clinical Psychology*. 1981;37(2): 451–455.
6. Abel G, Osborn C. Cognitive-behavioral Treatment of Sexual Misconduct. In: Bloom J, Nadelson C, Notman M. (eds.). *Physician Sexual Misconduct*. (pp. 225-246). Washington, DC: American Psychiatric Press:1999.
7. Tyrer P, Mulder R, Crawford M, et. al. Personality Disorder: A New Global Perspective. *World Psychiatry*. 2010;9(1):56–60.
8. Ronningstam E. Narcissistic Personality Disorder: Facing DSM-V. *Psychiatric Annals*. 2009;39:111-121.

CHAPTER 10

Rehabilitation of the Impaired Physician

"I have come to believe that hard times are not just meaningless suffering and that something good might turn up at any moment. That's a big change for someone who used to come to in the morning feeling sentenced to another day of life. When I wake up today, there are lots of possibilities. I can hardly wait to see what's going to happen next."

– ALCOHOLICS ANONYMOUS

AS I ROSE OVER THE top of the hill, the soft, glowing red lights on top of the Golden Gate Bridge slowly dimmed and brightened in my windshield. I gently pumped the brakes and rolled slowly downhill on Fillmore Street in San Francisco.

I was a first-year medical student, away from home in a foreign environment headed toward an Adult Children of Alcoholics (ACOA) meeting. A spin-off 12-step program from Alcoholics Anonymous, ACOA, founded in the 1970s, sought to help adults who were raised by alcoholic parents in dysfunctional families. As I entered the building, a few of the attendees were out smoking cigarettes — a familiar sight to me, as I had accompanied my mother to dozens of Alcoholics Anonymous meetings as a teenager in the 1980s.

It was my turn to make sense of my past, put it in perspective, and positively address some of the holdover effects of being raised in an alcoholic household. I had a lot of work to do, as the psychiatrist in student health referred me, a first-year medical student diagnosed with panic disorder and PTSD from childhood trauma, to a counselor and ACOA.

121

Despite this challenge, I thrived in medical school and continued getting counseling through residency. After nearly eight years of treatment, I said my goodbyes to my counselor and moved on. Not all of us have the courage to overcome the potential stigma of seeking treatment, and the only reason I am telling this story is to encourage others to seek treatment. Unresolved issues or untreated mental disorders do not disappear as medical students transition through residency and finally, practice as attending physicians. In fact, left untreated, the journey is much more difficult, and in my opinion, leads to unnecessary and needless suffering.

Physicians are reluctant to seek help, and this contributes to higher rates of suicide, substance abuse, divorce, and a host of other problems. State medical boards often ask intrusive questions regarding a physician's history of being treated for mental health disorders.[1] It is intuitively obvious an untreated mental health disorder can contribute to disruptive behaviors, and there are other barriers and reasons physicians do not seek treatment:[2]

1. Physician personality and characteristics, including doubt, guilt, and an exaggerated sense of responsibility.
2. Programmed to cope alone. Physicians are increasingly isolated in larger health systems and groups with production pressures. Physicians now spend more time documenting notes in the EMR, leading to burnout and screen fatigue.
3. Survivor mentality. Physicians endure both physical and emotional exhaustion in medical school and residency. This chronic cycle of exhaustion seemingly never ends and often extends into their practice after residency — leading some 37% of physicians to look forward to retirement as a strategy for well-being.
4. Self-doubt and imposter syndrome. Physicians do not want to appear 'weak' and insecure.

Physicians referred to formal rehabilitation programs for behavior or substance abuse disorders are either self-referred or, more commonly, mandated to participate in a program. Physicians mandated to participate in a professional behavior program often have a significant, long-standing history of behaviors, and participation in a formal program is a last resort to save a physician's career.

DRUG AND ALCOHOL USE DISORDERS

Alcohol use disorder (AUD) is a serious public health problem in the United States, and the annual costs for treating AUD and related health conditions is in the billions of dollars. Only recently has there been growing interest in surveying and identifying AUD in the physician population.[3] In 2015, nearly 28,000 physicians were invited to participate in a survey on substance use disorders (SUD) using validated instruments. Only 7,000 responded, but the results are alarming. Nearly 13% of male physicians and 21.4% of female physicians met diagnostic criteria for alcohol abuse or dependence.[3] Prescription and illicit drug use was rare.

Not surprisingly, surgeons had the highest rates of AUD at 15.4%.[4] Female surgeons had rates of 25%. Emotional exhaustion and deperson-alization domains associated with burnout were strongly associated with AUD. Surgeons who reported a major medical error in the previous three months were also more likely to have AUD. Throughout the past decade, physician burnout prevalence has increased, and the rates are likely higher. The prognosis for physicians undergoing treatment is high, but many physicians are reluctant to seek assistance.[1] Although not mentioned, some of the physicians with AUD also have untreated mood and anxiety disorders compounding the problem.

AUD contributes to the higher suicide rates of physicians compared to the general population. There is a 40% and 130% higher rate of suicide among male and female physicians, respectively, compared to the general population. Substance use disorder, including prescription drug use, is five times higher than the general population, and anesthesiologists have the highest rates of opioid use due to easy access.[5,6]

Several of my colleagues throughout the past decade have confiden-tially and voluntarily entered treatment programs. Each one recognized the problem and appropriately sought treatment. They had insight into how alcoholism was affecting their personal and/or professional lives and performance. With the renewed emphasis on safety and quality in patient care, it is clear impaired physicians make medical mistakes — some of which can lead to patient harm. With the physician shortage an acute issue facing the U.S. healthcare system, we cannot afford to ignore the impact of SUD and AUD.

DECIDING WHETHER TO REFER A COLLEAGUE TO A PHYSICIAN HEALTH PROGRAM

When a physician is suspected of having AUD or SUD, the ramifications are far-reaching. We have a responsibility to act in the best interest of our colleagues and patients. If we are incorrect and report a colleague, we have unduly burdened the physician and created an atmosphere of suspicion with both economic, professional, and personal consequences. Failure to act, however, also carries risk. Referring a colleague is serious and should never be taken lightly.[7]

The recommendations for a physician who suspects a colleague of AUD or SUD are straightforward. The AMA *Code of Medical Ethics* outlines the process:

> *Physicians' responsibilities to colleagues who are impaired by a condition that interferes with their ability to engage safely in professional activities include timely intervention to ensure that these colleagues cease practicing and receive appropriate assistance from a physician health program (PHP) ... Ethically and legally, it may be necessary to report an impaired physician who continues to practice despite reasonable offers of assistance and referral to a hospital or state physician health program. The duty to report ... may entail ... reporting to the licensing authority.[7]*

The challenge is ensuring there is a problem. For example, in the case when my colleague performed an anesthetic while impaired, I had to ask him open-ended questions. Was he tired, as he stated? I did not suspect fatigue — especially given his prior history of treatment for AUD. Is your colleague irritable because of a stressful home life, or is it a substance use issue? In these cases, it is not entirely clear how best to perform our ethical duty to promote good and prevent harm.

Our own objectivity might be compromised. What if a physician is referring a competitor to a program? What if we stand to gain something if a physician is referred? I mention these situations because other motives may be at play, even in a subtle fashion, if a colleague refers another colleague. Certainly, false claims have been made against physicians, and this falls under the umbrella of disruptive behavior. However, it is exceptionally difficult to prove intent.

We have a *prima facie* duty to respect the autonomy of physicians, but this duty can and should get trumped by other more pressing needs if we suspect that a physician is actively misusing substances or alcohol. Our duty to promote both beneficence and nonmaleficence has to trump the physician's right to autonomy. Furthermore, patients have a right to receive care from a physician who is not impaired.

Intervening requires a preponderance of evidence. Erratic behavior, poor clinical decision making, chronic tardiness, disheveled appearances, etc., are concerning, and this is especially true if the physician's behavior is new. The evidence must be examined within the overall context of the situation.

PHYSICIAN HEALTH PROGRAMS

Nearly all states have physician health programs (PHPs), and they can be self-referred, or a physician leader such as the CMO or Chief of Staff can also refer the physician. State medical boards can also mandate an impaired physician participate in a program. Substance use disorder treatment programs often require a 30- to 90-day treatment program. Unfortunately, these treatment programs often are not covered by health insurance. This can place an enormous economic burden on the physician, as there is both lost income while in treatment, and the expense of the programs.

Once completed, the physicians often enter monitoring agreements for a set period of time with random drug tests. Either the CMO or other designated physician leader will be responsible for ensuring the physician is compliant with all requirements during the monitoring agreement. My colleague successfully completed a monitoring agreement and continuing treatment with a substance use psychiatrist. Once complete, he relapsed without our knowledge. Unfortunately, there is not much we can do to ensure the physician remains sober after the monitoring agreement. There are numerous PHPs, and due to the rapid change in programs, it is recommended to ask the appropriate state medical board for current guidance.

Changing behavior requires genuine peer support and guidance. It is easy to fall into the trap the process is designed to punish the attributed physician. Resist this temptation. Part of creating a "just" culture and collaborative environment fosters support for physicians, nurses, and staff. Empathy and compassion are part of providing great patient care with quality outcomes.

Be willing to use your empathy and compassion toward your colleagues who are struggling. They deserve an opportunity to remediate themselves. Regardless of who we are, we are all human and share similar needs and are vulnerable to all of the failings of what it means to be human. Kindness and respect will make this journey more pleasant, and you will make a difference.

REFERENCES

1. Mehata S, Edwards M. Suffering in Silence: Mental Health Stigma and Physicians' Licensing Fears. *The American Journal of Psychiatry Residents Journal.* 2019;13(11):2–4.

2. Berg S. 5 Reasons Physicians Are Less Likely to Seek Support. American Medical Association. July 30, 2018.

3. Oreskovich M, Shanafelt T, Dyrbye L, et al. The Prevalence of Substance Use Disorders in American Physicians. *American Journal of Addiction.* 2015;24(1): 30–38.

4. Oreskovich M, Kaups, K, Balch C, et. al. Prevalence of Alcohol Use Disorders Among American Surgeons. *Archives of Surgery, JAMA Surgery Network.* 2012;147(2): 168–174.

5. Kaliszewski M. Substance Abuse Among Doctors: Key Statistics & Rehab Options. *Blog. American Addiction Centers.* February 8, 2021.

6. Merlo L, Gold M. Prescription Opioid Abuse and Dependence Among Physicians: Hypothesis and Treatment. *Harvard Review of Psychiatry.* 2008;16(3): 181–94.

7. Boyd W. Deciding Whether to Refer a Colleague to a Physician Health Program. *AMA Journal of Ethics.* Viewpoint, October 2015.

CHAPTER 11

Preventing Physician Disruptive Behavior

True prevention is not waiting for bad things to happen,
it's preventing things from happening in the first place.

– Don McPherson

EFFECTIVE COMMUNICATION

Effective professional, courteous communication among all parties in a healthcare system helps create a positive culture. Face-to-face communication and conversation are the most effective means to communicate our emotions, intent, and message. Our facial expressions, tone of voice, body language, and words deliver our messaging. Phone calls, too, are effective, as our tone of voice and cadence communicate the intent and tone of the message.

We live in a busy world with a lot of demands for our time and attention. Regardless, the seven basic characteristics for effective communication have not changed (Figure 1):

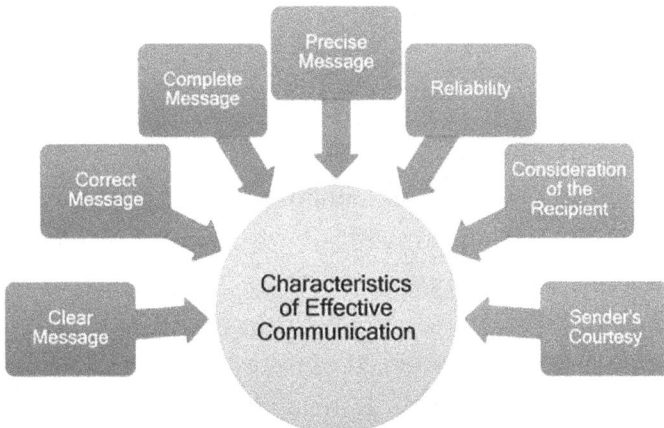

FIGURE 1. Characteristics of Effective Communication

Active listening is one of the most important ways to build trust and relationships. To ensure you interpret the message correctly, repeat what you think the speaker is communicating. It is remarkably easy to do. Just say, "What I hear you saying is.... and as a result of....... this happens. Is that correct?" It validates that you listened.

The communication process loop (Figure 2) is remarkably simple, but upon further examination, it is easy to see where, when, and how communication breakdowns can occur. Did the sender send the correct message? Did the receiver interpret the message correctly? Depending on the channel or medium, the velocity of the message may impact the effectiveness. For example, texts are faster than e-mails, but there are lots of opportunities for error and/or misinterpretation.

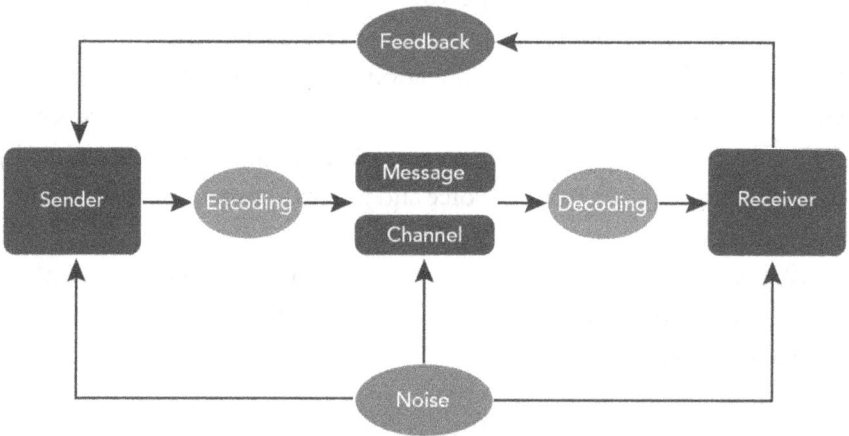

FIGURE 2. Communication Process Loop

Technology allows us to work around these older methods of communication. In the 1990s, e-mails provided a means for rapid communication among multiple parties and groups. It was a radical new way to disseminate large volumes of information quickly. Texting is now ubiquitous, and the technology is nearly 30 years old. The first text was sent by Neil Papworth in the UK on December 3, 1992. By the end of the first decade of the 21st century, texting was the norm, and it remains a popular method to rapidly communicate small bits of information.

Unfortunately, our social norms and etiquette have not adapted as quickly as our technological capabilities. Think three times before hitting "send" on the e-mail. Look three times before sending a text. The subtle message modifiers are absent. The intent of the message may be lost. The tone may not convey how you want the message to be perceived. The digital world is filled with traps and opportunities for error, and in a busy hospital where rapid communication between nurses, physicians, and all other support staff is required, the method of communicating can erode morale.

Here are some examples that I call "setups" for unprofessional conduct. An intensivist is on-call for the unit, and his pager or phone notifies him of a new page: *new admit.*

This page communicates the barest amount of information possible. All we know is there is a patient in the ER who is critically ill. There is no call back number, no attending identified — nothing. How do you think receiving a page like this makes the on-call physician feel? Is it respectful? What if the message stated this instead?:

Dr. Jones has a new admit. Please call 5623.

Think about the workflow of a busy intensivist. Now, all he has to do is pick up the phone, call Dr. Jones, and get the story. It is effective and professional, and it does not delay patient care. The page or text is much more respectful.

This example may seem trivial, but in a high-stress world with time pressures and multiple tasks, little jabs and barbs begin to take a toll. In larger institutions, short communications are often the norm, and with it, occasionally, a tone of disrespect can set in. Part of medical training is developing professional behaviors conducive to effective communication with others in a high-stress environment. Therefore, the environment can foment and create conditions ripe for rude phone calls, frustrated colleagues, and a toxic atmosphere.

As a practicing physician for 20 years, I have never regretted picking up the telephone or scheduling an in-person meeting. I have regretted sending e-mails and texts. You probably have to, and it is hard to walk back written words. Open lines of communication with proper dissemination using an appropriate medium help set up up a professional, communicative environment.

MANAGING AND MINIMIZING DRAMA IN THE WORKPLACE

Minimizing drama in the workplace is a significant challenge. Gossip is ubiquitous and occurs in all organizations. One or two employees who are prone to gossip, backstab, complain, and stir the pot can disrupt all efforts to create a professional, friendly, respectful work atmosphere. Understanding what drives gossip is necessary to reduce the negative impact in the work environment.

Gossip is broadly defined as simple, informal communication shared between two or more individuals about an individual who is not present. It is implied that the messages and information shared is usually negative in nature, and the amount of gossip in an organization increases the likelihood there is a culture of mistrust and poor morale.[1] This leads to lower productivity and erodes the organization's mission or purpose. In healthcare, these behaviors can indirectly impact patient care.

There are several theories about why people are motivated to gossip. It is multi-factorial, and as early as 1937, Herskovits suggested gossip serves as a means for an individual to broadcast personal judgments to others. Through broadcasting a judgment about another individual, we can quickly identify if others agree with us through either discussion or body language. Another reason people might gossip is to obtain information and achieve personal gain.[2] More recently, Noon and Delbridge argue that gossip involves a power-play as gossipers are able to achieve dominance or self-promotion.[3] Positive gossip or communication shared between individuals that is positive can lead to group cohesion and improved morale. Engaging in gossip requires a high degree of interpersonal trust and personal loyalty.[2,4]

There are specific strategies to reduce negative workplace gossip:

1. Set an example as a physician leader. Do not engage, encourage, or listen to gossip.

2. Cultivate an honest and open work environment by discussing issues when all involved parties are present.

3. Pay attention to the conditions under which gossip occurs. Clarifying underlying concerns and providing accurate information will diffuse negative gossip and place the focus on problem solving.

4. Maintain open, straightforward, and productive discussion of organizational changes or problems.

5. Utilize all means of communication, including frequent meetings, e-mails, bulletin boards, and keep lines of communication open.
6. Promptly and publicly correct misinformation or rumors.

Although it is tempting to have a zero-tolerance policy regarding gossip, it is not practical or realistic to expect all gossip to disappear. The point is to minimize the amount of gossip, contain its negative effects, and consistently and proactively address any root causes.

Another strategy is addressing the behavior with colleagues who regularly engage in gossip. In my experience, one or two members of a team regularly engage in gossip. If it is destructive, have a professional conversation regarding the corrosive nature of their behavior. As a department head or chair, you have to model the behavior and set expectations. *You will observe the behaviors you tolerate or model.* Set the bar high.

Another way to avoid drama is to not hire problematic physicians. During the hiring process, it is often easy to identify if a physician has a history of professional behavior or clinical quality concerns. Credentialing committees have a responsibility to do due diligence. How many different jobs has the physician had over the last decade? Has there been a long tenure in one practice?

During the interview process, it is also OK to ask how a physician handled a stressful situation. The answer will help guide you to making sound judgments. Do not willingly hire a problem physician who you know has a past history of behavioral issues.

ENVIRONMENTAL FACTORS AND STRESS

Our physical work environment affects our mood, productivity, and overall sense of well-being. Where we work impacts how we function and respond in the environment. High acuity areas and procedural areas of the hospital often generate more professional behavior complaints. Outpatient clinics have the least, and this makes sense.

Hospitals are open 24/7, and late at night or early in the morning, staff are fatigued, and with fatigue, the capacity to handle stress decreases. Some areas of the hospital are inherently high stress, including the ER, OR, ICU, and OB wards, and this contributes to the higher incidence and prevalence of disruptive behaviors for surgical, high acuity, and procedural medical specialties.

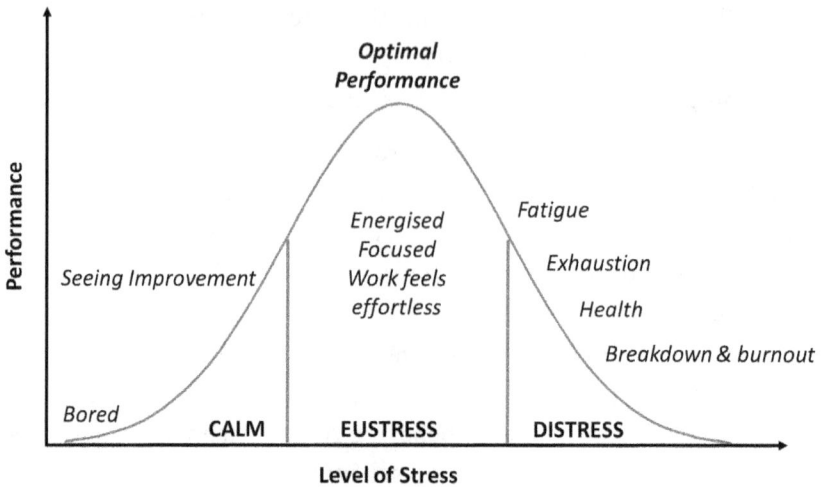

FIGURE 3. Levels of Stress

Chronic, high-stress work environments combined with long work hours contribute to burnout as well (Figure 3). Optimal conditions occur when the level of stress experienced is manageable and allows work tasks to be performed as expected. Physician burnout is directly correlated to work hours — the longer the workday or workweek, the higher likelihood a physician will have symptoms of burnout.[5]

As physicians lose autonomy as employees, they may lose control in managing a realistic work/life balance. As physician shortages continue, there is increased demand for services. Providing flexible scheduling, part-time work, and adequate paid time off or vacation help reduce physicians' feeling that they are overworked, which leads to distress and burnout.

PHYSICIAN SPECIALTIES AND DISRUPTIVE BEHAVIOR

It is difficult to quantify and qualify the exact number of behavior concerns and specialties represented because a majority of the complaints are kept confidential and rarely result in loss of privileges or become reportable events to the medical boards or National Practitioner Data Bank (NPDB). However, in my experience, specialists in high acuity practice environments are more prone to problematic behaviors. These locations include the emergency departments, operating rooms, labor wards, and intensive care units. These areas of the hospital are "high stakes," high-stress environments where critically ill patients place enormous pressure on everyone involved in providing care in these settings. The "pump," so to speak, is already primed.

Despite my biased observations, I am aware physicians from all specialties are represented. Knowing these practice areas are conducive to misconduct is helpful. In the case studies discussed earlier, a surgeon was upset that an instrument tray did not contain items necessary for the procedure. From the physician's perspective, these lapses can impact patient care, and yes, the surgeon has every right to be frustrated and angry — especially if it seems to be an ongoing problem. This is why, in the letter to the surgeon, I stated the committee would address this issue.

Hospital administrators and managers must be held accountable for these lapses and accept full responsibility for correcting or addressing real concerns or issues. Having a surgeon ask for a problem to be addressed for a third, fourth, or fifth time is simply unacceptable.

The OR is a unique environment with its own culture. The staff within the walls of each OR has clearly defined roles and responsibilities, and the surgeon historically is the so-called captain of the ship. A good working relationship between all parties in the OR is critical to avoid errors and provide excellent care.

With the surgeon perceived as the leader, everyone else is automatically the "subordinate," including, and some may disagree, the anesthesiologist or CRNA. It is easy to understand how two physicians in a high-stakes environment providing care for the same patient in different capacities is the ultimate setup for conflict. When the fertilizer hits the oscillator, there can be a bit of mudslinging across the blue surgical drape. A blame game can ensue either during or after surgery. The surgeon and anesthesiologist have a duty to create a civil and respectful OR environment where team members feel safe to speak out about safety concerns without fear of an outburst.

Physicians who are leaders in other clinic-based specialties need to understand the culture of the OR to understand the stress. Conversely, physicians from procedural-based specialties need to understand the unique stresses of hospitalists and clinic-based physicians who often have tremendous time pressures placed on them in high volume work environments. Stress is stress, but the type and frequency of stress creates different environments for physicians. When physicians from different specialties acknowledge the unique stresses of their colleague's practices, it helps create understanding and mutual trust.

360 FEEDBACK AND PERFORMANCE EVALUATIONS

Traditional annual employee evaluations usually include one-sided feedback from a manager or other senior executive and the employee. In a medical setting, these types of evaluations have limited utility and are being replaced by 360 Feedback evaluations in which employees are evaluated by peers and superiors using questionnaires.

360 reviews combine the perspectives of a manager and several peers about the teamwork, communication, leadership potential, and management skills of an employee. The reviewers are asked to comment and rate the employee's professional skills and team impact. Despite some criticism on the effectiveness of these evaluations, I think there is value when employees receive feedback comments that are consistent.

For example, if several peers rate an employee as "unapproachable," the employee is made aware of a problem. At this point, specific coaching or techniques can be offered to the employee. 360 Feedback is not meant to be punitive; therefore, it is important to communicate to all employees that the goal is to identify areas of weakness and also areas of strength so there can be meaningful improvement. Receiving positive feedback makes an employee feel valued and respected, and it is foundational for helping create a "just culture," which I discuss in the next section.

CONFLICT MANAGEMENT

Conflict will always exist, as individuals, groups, and organizations often have competing interests. Conflict can be managed constructively or destructively. Destructive conflict creates a negative work environment through erosion of team performance, trust, and collaboration. What makes conflict in healthcare particularly challenging is the fact most care environments achieve the work either through structured teams or "pseudo" teams.

For example, the operating room is a highly matrixed team with staff who have clearly identified roles and responsibilities. A pseudo team might be composed of a nurse, hospitalist, and consultant physician. Pseudo teams are informal, fluid; the members of the team may come and go. In addition, they may or may not work together in the same environment at the same time.

Conflict occurs in three fundamental domains: individual, interpersonal, and organizational. Individual conflicts arise when the individual's concept of self is challenged or threatened by others' disagreement. Consequences include the possibility of misinterpreting others' motives, world views, or abilities as flawed.[6] Interpersonal conflict is often created after a breakdown in communication or if two parties have competing interests. Organizational conflict occurs when resources are scarce, there is competition, or if workflow processes, policies, tasks, and procedures are not clearly defined.[6]

An individual's, group's, or organization's response to conflict and how conflict is managed are critical to creating a professional, courteous, respectful environment. Avoiding conflict, or worse, ignoring it exists, is a perfect setup for passive-aggressive behaviors, gossip, and distrust. This environment is primed for an escalation in professional conduct issues. Many unresolved issues or concerns can create a codependent environment where all individuals and teams function in a dysfunctional environment, accommodating the problems in inconsistent patterns of behavior. This is how organizations can quickly fail and fall apart.

As a leader, you will develop your own leadership style, as previously discussed. Having an awareness of the five conflict management styles is essential in effectively resolving conflict proactively with positive outcomes.

The five conflict management styles are competing, avoiding, compromising, collaborating, and accommodating. As shown in Figure 4, the Y-axis represents assertiveness, and the X-axis, cooperativeness. In an ideal world, all conflicts would be resolved quickly with a collaborative approach.[7]

There are different circumstances and situations when each conflict management style is most effective. Accommodating conflict management is effective when you set aside your own needs and focus on others' needs. This is a useful approach when you are wrong or do not have as much at stake, and when there is no point in arguing. Do not misinterpret this style as "weak." For example, if you are wrong and are willing to admit it, or if a colleague is wrong and willing to admit it, this is a behavior that creates and builds trust.

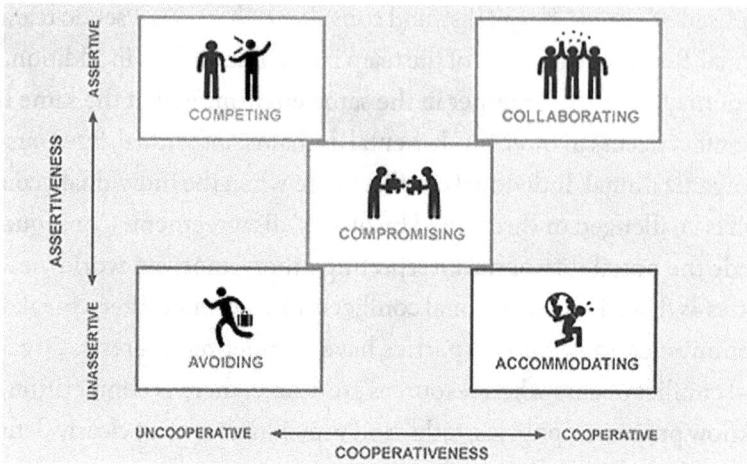

FIGURE 4. Conflict Management Styles

Compromising conflict styles partially satisfy both parties. Both sides must give a little to arrive at a solution. This strategy is useful when reaching a solution is more important than the solution itself, when you need a temporary solution, and when there seems to be an impasse. It is important to note that compromising solutions can be *temporary* if there is a limited resource that will be addressed or if another project has priority. If the compromise is a permanent solution, be aware any new stressors or changes to the agreed-upon solution can lead to more conflict.

Collaborating conflict management is a win-win for all parties. A solution has been created that satisfies all interests, and there is a sense of harmony. This is especially important if the relationships and solutions will have a large and significant impact on the organization or to a large group of stakeholders.

Competing styles utilize the headstrong approach without any compromise. This style is useful when your personal beliefs, values, and needs are at risk. This style is also a "last resort" when all other styles have failed. Lastly, avoiding conflict styles ignores the conflict. This style is useful if the conflict is meaningless or you do not know enough information to address the issue. This approach is often temporary and sometimes delays the inevitable reemergence or continuance of the conflict. Be careful using this strategy, as it is the least effective.

Regardless of the style used to manage conflict, embracing conflict and knowing it is an expected byproduct of growth and change will help you keep your sanity. Effective conflict management strategy is an essential skill of great physician leaders. Lastly, recognize that conflict itself is not disruptive behavior, but disruptive behavior can arise out of conflict.

Case Example

As Chair of the Surgical Executive Committee, I was tasked with managing OR block times, process improvement strategies and efforts, etc. The fun part of the job was creating and finishing projects or working on improving patient care with various initiatives. However, I was blindsided with an issue between two surgeons who had a conflict on resource utilization.

The hospital had recently constructed a "hybrid" OR with state-of-the-art imaging capabilities and a video system for complex vascular and non-invasive cardiac procedures. The intent for the hybrid room was to provide the vascular surgeons better imaging; however, a cardiac surgeon wanted to use the room because it also had a state-of-the-art video system that displayed the surgeon's point of view on screens on the wall.

It was not necessary to have this option to improve clinical care, but the surgeon felt the other team members would know what is going on with a better look during surgery. This made sense. The vascular surgeons wanted the use of the room four days per week, leaving a solo block time on Friday afternoons for cardiac cases.

Two competing groups wanted access to a limited resource. That was the setup. To add another element to this vignette, the cardiac surgeon and the Chair of Vascular Surgery did not care for each other personally. The conflict was complicated by this emotional component. Hospital administration offered to allocate a six-figure sum to build a new video system in a different room. The vascular surgeon felt this was a waste of capital, and there were other more pressing needs in the OR. This was a true statement. Other projects would be delayed.

I had two groups who had personal animosity toward each other competing for a limited resource. What to do?

As Chair of the Surgical Executive Committee, I had the authority to make a unilateral recommendation to approve or disapprove the capital spend. I felt this route would not satisfy everyone involved, so my proposal was simple. I invited each surgeon to present a pro or con case in front of the committee. After discussion, we would vote on the proposal and let them know of our decision.

This decision gave the opposing parties a voice to make their case in front of an impartial committee. It allowed for a discussion with more than two or three individuals, including the CEO and CFO. And the decision could not be 'pinned' on one individual.

After the presentations, the committee decided to approve the spend with the belief it had some clinical utility and other surgeons may find the system useful as well. Additionally, I was able to maintain a respectful, professional relationship with both surgeons. The lesson learned is to be objective and fair as much as possible.

PREVENTING SEXUAL HARASSMENT

Sexual harassment in healthcare is just as prevalent as it is in other industries, and as part of an onboarding process, most organizations require formal training programs educating employees on the definitions of sexual harassment and how to report the behavior. In 1980, the EEOC released guidance on sexual harassment training, and nearly 75% of corporations and mid-sized businesses now incorporate formal sexual harassment training. Unfortunately, the EEOC released a report in 2016 with findings suggesting these programs fail at prevention due in large part because most of the programs focus on the legal liabilities and implications. In other words, these programs are largely ineffective.

A study by Sitzmann and Weinhardt confirms that training program effectiveness is measured through a reduction in undesirable legal outcomes.[8] Given the high cost of legal actions, sexual harassment training costs are justified as a business investment; however, this is short-sighted. The primary focus for effective training should be to create a culture that does not tolerate sexual harassment in any form — the legal liability will take care of itself in a "just culture."

Rather than focus on training, enforcing a zero-tolerance policy may be more effective in reducing sexual harassment.[9] Given the paucity of research on the effectiveness of sexual harassment training, perhaps a proactive approach is to provide the training, include the expectations in a code of conduct, and finally, have a near zero-tolerance policy.

More recently, a new approach to training has proven effective in the military and on college campuses. Bystander training includes specific actions and behaviors for bystanders who witness sexual harassment to intervene proactively rather than freeze in fear. The bystander effect is a social psychological theory that individuals are less likely to intervene when others are present. Intervening works during a witnessed event, but many forms of sexual harassment take place when the victim and perpetrator are alone.

An additional problem impeding progress in reducing sexual harassment is victims' lack of faith in grievance procedures. There is a real fear of retaliation or lack of support. Title VII protects employees from retaliation when reporting sexual harassment, but why should victims be subject to a system that makes a bad situation worse through retaliation or ignoring the claim? Nurses, in fact, have been fired for reporting sexual harassment.[10]

In summary, there is no "magic bullet" to create an environment entirely free of sexual harassment. Instead of focusing on avoiding the negative economic and legal consequences of sexual harassment, organizations should create a culture of awareness of the problem with clear expectations and consequences for violating policy. Current efforts are moving in the right direction, but in my opinion, not quickly enough.

CREATING A JUST CULTURE

Creating a "just culture" is a significant challenge. A just culture is an organization embracing principles of fairness, justice, and respectful, professional behavior. Just cultures recognize the importance of transparency and openness.[11] Institutions cannot create a just culture without reducing and properly handling disruptive behaviors, and physician leaders have a responsibility to help lead transformative efforts toward openness and transparency. Promoting professionalism is an unwritten rule for all leaders, but it is especially important for physician leaders in a high-stress environment.

There are five guiding principles to help establish a just culture[12]:

1. Promoting justice.
2. Freedom from conflicts of interest.
3. Obtaining reasonable certainty about system failures and individual performance problems.

4. Providing meaningful feedback or disciplinary measures that maximize the recipient's likelihood of gaining insight.
5. Conducting disciplinary actions conducive to restoring a colleague to responsible, teamwork promoting professionalism and disengaging from those unwilling or unable to change.

Justice means, at a basic level, treating others as you want to be treated. To accomplish this, there must be strict adherence to organizational conduct policies and other documents such as the medical staff bylaws. Conflicts of interest (COI) can derail your efforts and create distrust. COI must be identified and voluntarily addressed. Real or perceived COI may 'disqualify' a leader from participating in investigating or chairing proceedings, interventions, or meetings. Recusing yourself from certain incidents due to COI is your responsibility.

Reasonable certainty means the events or behavior described or reported is valid and not based on hearsay. Gossip is not good enough, nor is a second- or third-hand account of an event. Earlier I discussed the importance of witnesses. When two or more individuals can attest to witnessing an event, it is likely valid.

Helping colleagues achieve insight into their behavior is one of the goals of corrective action and intervention. In my experience, physicians who acknowledge their role in the problem are usually cognizant and aware and, more importantly, learn from their mistakes and move on. The incident is one and done. Without this insight, there is often no lasting change.

Redemption, restoration or return to professional behavior is the final guiding principle and desired outcome. If efforts fail to achieve this goal, the final disposition may be termination or loss of privileges. This is a last resort, but as I have repeated many times, allowing professional misconduct to continue will not allow the healthcare organization to accomplish most of its goals to create safer, higher-quality outcomes.

The physicians, nurses, and other staff need to feel safe reporting unprofessional conduct without fear of retribution — either laterally, from superiors, or from subordinates. Organizations that have designed anonymous reporting systems are best positioned to protect the individual making the report. Fear of retribution and reciprocity continues.

Despite efforts to develop a just culture, hospitals continue to struggle with staff who are afraid to report safety incidents.[13] A culture of blame still exists in most organizations, and I think what continues to drive this culture is that it is easier to address the issue with one individual rather than do a deep dive and *change* the system. Creating a just culture is a process itself that happens over time with continued practice, and it is an infinite process with no end.

HIGH-RELIABILITY ORGANIZATIONS AND DISRUPTIVE BEHAVIOR

It is impossible for an organization to achieve high reliability if disruptive behaviors are not addressed. There are five principles guiding high-reliability organizations (HROs): preoccupation with failure, reluctance to simplify, sensitivity to operations, commitment to resilience, and deference to expertise.[14] These five pillars provide support to the concept that HROs recognize that systemic failures lead to errors. In other words, competent and skilled physicians and nurses can make mistakes in poorly designed systems. This explains the high rate of wrong-site surgery. Nearly 100 wrong-site surgeries are performed annually in the US. This is a rate of twice per week and should be "never" events.[15]

In response, the universal protocol suggested by Atul Gawande, calls for a "time out" prior to the start of the procedure. The elements of the time out include site marking after identifying the right patient and confirming the side or level of surgery or the type of procedure. I have taken part in this process for years, and I have witnessed surgeons choose not to participate or participate minimally in this process. This is disruptive behavior. It sets a precedent contrary to HRO principles and reinforces a double standard in behavioral expectations, etc.

Changing the culture from a traditional approach of blaming individuals for errors and recognizing the significant contributions from workplace processes and systems takes time, money, and resources. The transformative change is slow, and there can be stubborn resistance from some staff. Allowing disruptive behaviors to continue unaddressed, or worse, inconsistently enforcing the code of conduct will derail organizational efforts to achieve high reliability.

REFERENCES

1. Burke L, Wise J. The Effective Care, Handling, and Pruning of the Office Grapevine. *Business Horizons.* 2003:46:71–76.

2. Luna A, Chou S. Drivers for Workplace Gossip: An Application of the Theory of Planned Behavior. *Journal of Organizational Culture, Communications, and Conflict.* 2013;17(1):115–129.

3. Noon M, Delbridge R. News from Behind My Hand: Gossip in Organizations. *Organizational Studies.* 1993;14(1):23–36.

4. Grosser T, Lopez-Kidwell V, Labianca G. A Social Network Analysis of Positive and Negative Gossip in Organization Life. *Group and Organization Management.* 2010;35(2):177–212.

5. Peckham C. Medscape National Physician Burnout & Depression Report 2019. *Medscape.* 2019. Retrieved April 12, 2021, from /www.medscape.com/slideshow/2019-lifestyle-burnout-depression-6011056#2.

6. Kim S, Bochatay N, Relyea-Chew A, et. al. Individual, Interpersonal, and Organizational Factors of Healthcare Conflict: A Scoping Review. *Journal of Interprofessional Care.* 2017;31(3):282-290.

7. Novak M. 5 Most Effective Conflict Management Styles (+When To Use Each One). *Learn Hub.* May 14, 2019. Retrieved from https://learn.g2.com/conflict-management-styles.

8. Sitzmann T, Weinhardt J. Training Engagement Theory: A Multilevel Perspective on the Effectiveness of Work-related Training. *Journal of Management.* Published online November 30, 2017.

9. Williams J, Fitzgerald L, Drasgow F. The Effects of Organizational Practices on Sexual Harassment and Individual Outcomes in the Military. *Military Psychology.* 1999;11(3):303–328.

10. OSD Staff. Was Nurse Fired for Reporting a Sexual Assault? *Outpatient Surgery.* News Bulletin. June 17, 2014.

11. Connor M, Duncombe D, Barclay E, et al. Creating a Fair and Just Culture: One Institution's Path Toward Organizational Change. *Joint Commission Journal on Quality and Patient Safety.* 2007;33(10):617–624.

12. Reiter C, Pichert J, Hickson G. Addressing Behavior and Performance Issues That Threaten Quality and Patient Safety: What Your Attorneys Want You to Know. *Progress in Pediatric Cardiology.* 2012;33:37–45.

13. Edwards M. An Assessment of the Impact of Just Culture on Quality and Safety in US Hospitals. *American Journal of Medical Quality.* 2018;33(5):502–508.

14. The Health Foundation. High Reliability Organizations. Website. November 2011.

15. Pelligrini C. Retained Foreign Bodies and Wrong Site Surgery Continue To Be a Challenge. *Bulletin of the American College of Surgeons.* December 4, 2019.

CHAPTER 12

Physician Burnout: Impact on Behavior

"Improvement usually means doing something that we have never done before."

– Shigeo Shingo

"A bad system will beat a good person every time."

– W E Deming

PHYSICIAN BURNOUT IS A COMBINATION of emotional exhaustion, depersonalization, and reduced personal accomplishment; the Maslach Burnout Inventory is a validated tool to assess the level of burnout in the workforce.[1] Over the last decade, the prevalence of physician burnout has skyrocketed.[2] The reasons are multi-factorial and include loss of autonomy, increased regulatory and compliance burdens, the electronic medical record, and an overall sense of powerlessness.

Highly trained physicians have been reduced to data-entry clerks, with more than 60% of most physicians' workday spent in front of a screen entering low-value administrative data.[3] A majority of the physician workforce is now employed by large national physician staffing companies, a hospital or hospital health system, and more recently, by health insurance companies. The era of the independent practitioner or shareholder in a private group is rapidly disappearing. A consequence is reduced control over the practice, work hours, and accommodation of work preferences. Physicians are disenfranchised, and many feel like they are "cogs on the wheel" of the vast machine of corporate medicine.

The consequences of burnout include increased medical errors, reduced productivity, and physicians choosing to leave the practice of medicine.[4,5] Emotional exhaustion leads to an increase in workplace violence, conflict, and disruptive behaviors.[5] The capacity for the physician to be adaptable or flexible and resilient is reduced in a burned-out physician. It makes intuitive sense that burned-out physicians have less reserve to function positively and respond to workplace stress. Feeling hopeless, it is easier to express frustration with coworkers or other staff.

Because the reasons for burnout are multi-factorial, there is no easy fix to reduce its incidence and prevalence. Some healthcare organizations are employing chief wellness officers tasked with addressing and creating solutions to the problem. This is a good first step, but alleviating burnout is a process, and it will take time to observe results.

REFERENCES

1. Schaufeli W, Bakker A, Hoogduin K, Schaap C, Kladler A. On the Clinical Validity of the Maslach Burnout Inventory and the Burnout Measure. *Psychology and Health.* 2001;16:656–582.
2. Shanafelt T, Hasan, Dyrbye L, Sinsky, C., Satele, D, et al. Changes in Burnout and Satisfaction with Work-life Balance in Physicians and the General US Working Population Between 2011-2014. *Mayo Clinic Proceedings.* 2015;90(12):600–613.
3. Downing I, Bates D, Longhurst C. Physician Burnout in the Electronic Health Record Era: Are We Ignoring the Real Cause? *Annals of Internal Medicine.* 2018;169(1):50–51.
4. Patel R, Bachu R, Adikey A, Malik M, Shah M. Factors Related to Physician Burnout and Its Consequences: A Review. *Behavioral Sciences.* 2018;8(98):1–7.
5. Shanafelt T & Noseworthy J. Executive Leadership and Physician Well-Being: Nine Organizational Strategies To Promote Engagement and Reduce Burnout. *Mayo Clinic Proceedings.* 2017;92(1):129–146.

CHAPTER 13

Moving Forward: Leadership Investment Strategies

Most of us lead far more meaningful lives than we know.

– Rachel Naomi Remen

I AM CONVINCED INVESTING IN AND encouraging physician leadership is an antidote to burnout and creates a positive, patient-centered healthcare system. Healthy and robust healthcare organizations are resilient and flexible, and a culture of respect can reduce professional misconduct not only among physicians but within the entire organization. It starts with awareness and acknowledgment, but that is not enough.

The physician leader's behaviors play a critical role in the behaviors of the physicians they lead.[1] Therefore, it is paramount to promote the appropriate physician leaders. Individuals who are engaged, listen, and have gained respect from their peers are malleable and open to change. Providing formal programs in leadership training to these physicians is an effective strategy. Lastly, regular evaluations of physician performance by those they lead should provide meaningful suggestions for improvement. Too many organizations measure leadership performance using financial metrics.

There is some evidence physician participation as members of the board of directors improves outcomes, and there is a paucity of research on whether physician-led and managed healthcare organizations perform better than non-physician-led organizations.[2] Nevertheless, physician-led organizations are uniquely positioned because a physician understands the clinical workflow and demands of fellow physicians. I suspect creating buy-in for change management and developing service lines and other programs to assist physicians is met with less resistance. Organizational changes in healthcare are more likely to succeed when healthcare professionals have the opportunity to influence the change, feel prepared for the change, and recognize the value of the change, including perceiving the benefit of the change for patients.[3]

Investing in leadership also sets organizations on a continued path toward success through succession planning. Leaders develop other leaders and encourage other physicians through mentorship and setting a positive example. In addition, medical schools are creating combined MD/MBA programs.[4] As healthcare finance and delivery have increasingly involved complicated reimbursement structures with an emphasis on quality and value, having detailed knowledge of the business processes gives physicians an opportunity to provide both clinical and business acumen in making decisions. Formally training leaders on managing conflict, negotiation, and professional behavior management would help leaders establish an effective, standardized approach.

REFERENCES

1. Shanafelt T, Noseworthy J. Executive Leadership and Physician Well-Being: Nine Organizational Strategies To Promote Engagement and Reduce Burnout. *Mayo Clinic Proceedings.* 2017;92(1):129–146.
2. Clay-Williams R, Ludlow K, Testa L, Li Z, Braithwhite J. Medical Leadership, A Systematic Narrative Review: Do Hospitals and Healthcare Organisations Perform Better When Led By Doctors? *BMJ Open.* 2017;7(9). Published online: doi: 10.1136/bmjopen-2016-014474
3. Nilsen P, Seeing I, Ericsson C, Birken S, Schildmeijer K. Characteristics of Successful Changes in Health Care Organizations: An Interview Study with Physicians, Registered Nurses, and Assistant Nurses. *BMC Health Services Research.* 2020;20:147.
4. Crocitto L, Kapoor D, Loughlin K. Development of Physician Leadership. *Urology Clinics of North America.* 2021;48(2):179–186.

CHAPTER 14

Conclusion

"The future depends on what we do in the present."

– MAHATMA GANDHI

" ... the powerful play goes on, and you will contribute a verse."

– WALT WHITMAN

I T IS MY HOPE THE cases and discussions have helped shed light and guidance on a difficult topic. I am optimistic about the future of medicine, and when I am asked if I would become a physician if I had to do it all over it again, my answer is a resounding yes. Practicing medicine and serving others is a blessing. The training is long and the work difficult, but worth it.

As more women become physicians, and as our physician workforce and leaders begin to truly reflect the vibrant diversity of our communities, we will continue to improve patient care. Unprofessional behavior, as many of the cases illuminated, is a response to a complex set of characteristics and environmental influences. We need to change the culture of medical training. We need to recognize the real human suffering of physicians as they bear witness, daily, to the suffering of others.

And as physicians, we need to ask ourselves and our colleagues how we can help each other as we walk the path of providing healing to others. We need to exercise the same compassion we feel for our patients toward ourselves and our colleagues.

Helping, fixing, and serving represent three ways of seeing life. When you help, you see life as weak. When you fix, you see life as broken. When you serve, you see life as whole. Fixing and helping may be the work of the ego, and service the work of the soul.

—*Rachel Naomi Remen*

147

APPENDIX

SAMPLE REPORT AND DISPOSITION FORM

St. Anywhere Hospital Professional Conduct Report and Disposition Form

Event Information:
Date of Occurrence: _____ Date Received: _____
Attributed Physician: _____ Department: _____

Conduct Concern:

Parties Involved:

Comments:

Intervention:
____Discussion with Department or Division Chair
____Meeting with CMO/President of Medical Staff
____Meeting with Professional Behavior Committee
____Immediate suspension of privileges

Disposition Options:
____No further follow-up. Resolved.
____Letter of Education/Recommendations
____Letter of Reprimand
____Professionalism CME/Education/Treatment Program
____Dismissal

After disposition is determined, immediately write a professional letter outlining the events of the meeting and disposition. Always keep your door open for further discussion or inquiry. Committee decisions help protect you from becoming "the bad cop" in the eyes of the medical staff.

PROFESSIONAL CONDUCT POLICY EXAMPLES

Employed Physician Example

Disruptive Behavior

I. Purpose of Policy

This policy affirms Alpha Healthcare System's commitment to attaining ever-increasing levels of excellence by establishing a just culture and an environment of safety, quality, professionalism, respect, collegiality, and teamwork at all times, prohibiting behaviors that undermine a safe and collegial environment, and identifying appropriate responses to such disruptive behaviors.

II. Policy Scope

This policy applies to the following positions at our four hospitals in Springfield County: Physicians/Fellows/Residents, Associate Providers, Non-Provider Staff, Temporary Staff, Per Diem/PRN Staff, Volunteers, Travelers, Students, Independent Contractors, and Leased Employees.

Nothing in this policy provides any contractual rights regarding employee privacy, nor does anything in this policy alter or modify the employment-at-will relationship between Alpha Healthcare Systems and its employees.

III. Definitions

Awareness Conversation: A conversation that any person can have with any other person in which the first describes an observed behavior by the latter that is not consistent with the standards and expectations for professional conduct described in the Code of Ethical Conduct. Awareness conversations may take place, for example, between physicians and/or staff, and other covered individuals including peers, co-workers, and colleagues, and do not have to be documented or reported.

Disruptive Behavior: Behavior that includes, but is not limited to, words or actions that create or have the potential to create an unsafe or hostile environment for patients, families, or other staff, to interfere with patient care, or to disrupt Alpha Healthcare System operations. It includes behavior that interferes with or undermines the level of teamwork and collegial respect that are critical to a safe environment. See the Appendix at the end of this policy for some specific examples of disruptive behaviors. Disruptive behavior includes "egregious behavior" as defined below.

Egregious Behavior: Highly offensive and/or aggressive acts (including those that could also constitute criminal acts such as assault or theft), discrimination, boundary violations, or working while under the influence of a substance or alcohol (refer to the Substance Abuse and Drug-Free Workplace Policy and the Fitness for Duty Policy).

IV. Policy Statement

Alpha Healthcare System is committed to excellence in patient care and to providing a healing environment for our patients and families and a safe and secure environment for our work force. The goal is to enable physicians and staff to attain ever-increasing levels of excellence by establishing environments of safety, quality, continuous learning, and accountability. As such, all physicians, and staff (and all others identified as "covered individuals" above) shall act in a professional, collaborative, and respectful manner at all times, consistent with applicable policies and procedures and the Code of Ethical Conduct. Alpha Healthcare System shall respond to all reported incidents of disruptive behavior in a manner intended to remedy the situation based on the particular facts and circumstances.

1. **Covered Individual Responsibility**
   - Each member of the Alpha Healthcare System community (to include all "covered individuals" identified above) is accountable for adhering to Alpha Healthcare System expectations of professional, respectful, and safe conduct. In addition, each member of the Alpha Healthcare System community is responsible for reporting incidents of disruptive behavior using the process outlined below.
   - When a covered individual observes another member of the community engaging in disruptive behavior that appears to be a first instance for which timely, direct feedback would likely prevent recurrence, and if the behavior or conduct is not egregious, the covered individual — if comfortable doing so — may, and is encouraged to, conduct an "awareness conversation" to address the behavior. Employees may contact Employee Relations for guidance and/or assistance with such discussions, or to request that the behavior be addressed by Employee Relations.

- If a covered individual chooses not to engage in an awareness conversation with the person engaging in disruptive behavior, the covered individual is strongly encouraged to report his or her observations using the process below.
- When a covered individual observes another member of the community engaging in disruptive behavior that the individual believes rises above minor instances of disruptive behavior or conduct (i.e., of the type appropriate for an awareness conversation), the covered individual is required to report the incident using the process outlined below.

2. **Reporting Disruptive Behavior**
   - Covered individuals are responsible for promptly reporting any disruptive behavior (other than minor instances as addressed above in Paragraph 1), including all instances of egregious behavior, by notifying or contacting the following:
     - A supervisor or any other person in management
     - Alpha Healthcare System's Occurrence or Incident Reporting System
     - Employee Relations at (123)-456-7890.
     - Alpha Healthcare System's Compliance Help Line at (123) 765-4321
   - In addition, if a covered individual is informed of an instance of disruptive behavior by a patient or visitor, the covered individual must inform his or her supervisor or other person in management at Alpha Healthcare System. Any reported incident of egregious behavior must be reported immediately.
   - The individual who is reporting a disruptive behavior incident may remain anonymous and will be asked to provide the following:
     - The date and time of the incident
     - The name of the person exhibiting disruptive behavior
     - Information about who was involved, including patients, if any, and the circumstances that precipitated the situation
     - A factual and objective description of the behavior
     - Identification of others who might have observed the incident
   - All reports will be treated as confidential to the greatest extent possible and consistent with applicable laws.

- If a behavior poses or appears to pose an immediate threat of harm to any individual, e.g., assault or threat of assault, or other behavior that may result in bodily harm, Alpha Healthcare System Security (when Security is available on site), or local law enforcement should be contacted.
- If a covered individual is concerned that his or her report has not been appropriately handled, he or she should contact Employee Relations or, if the event was reported to Employee Relations, the covered individual may contact his/her supervisor or the Office of General Counsel.

3. **Organizational Response**
   - Employee Relations or the department chair, as appropriate to the type of behavior at issue and the category of covered individual, will review each complaint of disruptive behavior and advise departmental leadership on the appropriate response based on the specific facts and circumstances.
   - Response to the disruptive behavior may take a variety of forms, including without limitation informal counseling, affirmation of expectations of employment, corrective action, performance improvement plan, fitness for duty evaluation, and disciplinary action up to and including immediate termination in accordance with Alpha Healthcare System policies and practices, and in accordance, as applicable, with the Alpha Healthcare System Professional Staff Bylaws.
   - Alpha Healthcare System takes egregious behaviors seriously and adopts a "zero tolerance" approach. Any egregious behavior may result in immediate dismissal from employment (subject, as applicable, to requirements for physicians and others Professional Staff members as set forth in the Alpha Healthcare System Professional Staff Bylaws, and to requirements for graduate medical education trainees set forth in applicable GME policies, including due process rights set forth therein) and reporting to applicable professional boards or regulatory agencies.
   - As may be appropriate depending on the specific facts and circumstances, resources which may be offered to help the employee

include but are not limited to Employee Relations or the Employee Assistance Program.

- All corrective action and disciplinary action will be taken in a manner consistent with the Corrective Action Policy and/or the Bylaws, Rules and Regulations of Alpha Healthcare System Professional Staff, as applicable.
- Documentation of the organizational response will be provided to the employee who was the subject of the review and a copy sent to Human Resources for inclusion in the employee file and/or included in the professional staff member credentialing file, maintained in the Medical Staff Office, as appropriate. Such documentation will be considered along with other feedback, in connection with an employee performance evaluation process and, with respect to professional staff members, in connection with the professional staff reappointment process and related credentialing and privileging processes. Employee Relations shall maintain documentation of all incidents of disruptive behavior investigated by Employee Relations, pursuant to Human Resources guidelines and practices.

4. **Employee Protection**
   - Alpha Healthcare System prohibits retaliation and will take no adverse action against any person for making a disruptive behavior report in good faith. Retaliation and adverse action in response to reporting any incident of disruptive behavior would include but are not limited to the following: discharge, demotion, suspension, harassment, denial of promotion, transfer or in any other manner discriminating or threatening to discriminate against an Alpha Healthcare System employee in the terms and conditions of the employee's employment.
   - Any employee who believes that he or she has been subjected to retaliatory conduct for reporting an incident of disruptive behavior may report the concern to Employee Relations at 123-4567, Compliance and Audit Services at (111) 222-3333 or the Compliance Helpline at (111) 444-5555 for timely investigation of such concern of retaliatory conduct.

5. **Examples of Disruptive Behaviors**
   The following list is a small subset of the types of behaviors and

communications that undermine a culture of safety and are in direct conflict with the Code of Ethical Conduct. These are examples and by no means meant to be an exhaustive list.

- Examples of overt disruptive behavior include:
  - Outbursts of anger, such as throwing instruments, charts, or other objects
  - Intimidation/threats
  - Unnecessary/inappropriate touching or contact
  - Harassment, innuendoes, or use of obscene gestures
  - Racial, ethnic, or sexual orientation jokes or comments
  - Unwillingness to adhere to section/department standards of practice or policies or refusing to perform assigned tasks
  - Frivolous, retaliatory, or intentionally misleading ("bad faith") reports of disruptive behavior or other policy violation
  - Use of derogatory or foul language
  - Inappropriate expressions of anger
  - Comments intended to undermine another physician, trainee, and/or staff member's self-confidence in providing care
  - Use of condescending or disrespectful language
  - Showing up to work impaired by alcohol or other substance
- Examples of covert disruptive behavior include repetitive instances of:
  - Unfair/unreasonable delegation of tasks or assignments (e.g., outside scope of practice or job description)
  - Sarcastic or impatient responses directed at another individual
  - Sabotage
  - Comments that undermine a patient's trust in other caregivers or the institution
  - Refusal to answer questions, respond to calls, or return pages in a timely manner

I AGREE TO ABIDE BY THE PROFESSIONAL BEHAVIOR EXPEC-TATIONS (CODE OF CONDUCT) OF **ALPHA HEALTH SYSTEMS** AND UNDERSTAND THAT CONDUCT BELOW THE STANDARDS SET FORTH HEREIN CAN RESULT IN DISCIPLINARY ACTION UP

TO AND INCLUDING THE TERMINATION OF MY PRIVILEGES
AND MEMBERSHIP ON THE MEDICAL STAFF.

_____ DATED THIS_____DAY
OF_____, 20___

APPLICANT'S SIGNATURE

Mixed Medical Staff Conduct Policy Example

Professional Behavior Expectations (Code of Conduct)

Purpose: The Code of Conduct sets expectations for high level professionalism and ethical conduct. The standards for behavior are provided under Principles. The Code of Conduct applies to all practicing professionals including, physicians, dentists, psychologists, and allied health professionals with membership or clinical privileges at Alpha Health System. Those with membership or clinical privileges are expected to adhere to the applicable Medical Staff Bylaws and Rules and Regulations.

Principles
Reasonable expectations for all practitioners include, by way of example, but are not limited to:

1. Supporting policies promoting cooperation, teamwork, and mutual respect among all members of the healthcare team.
2. Communicating with others in a clear and respectful manner.
3. Using conflict resolution skills in managing disagreements.
4. Addressing concerns about clinical judgments with appropriate Medical Center/Medical Staff personnel directly and privately.
5. Addressing dissatisfaction with policies through appropriate grievance channels.
6. Accepting appropriate feedback and demonstrating a change in behavior.
7. Completing medical records in a timely manner.
8. Respond to clinical obligations in a timely manner.
9. Complying with all applicable laws and regulations.

Behavior that unnecessarily impairs the efficient delivery of high-quality patient care is disruptive behavior and will be considered unacceptable

by Department Chairs, Credentials Committees, and Medical Executive Committees. Examples include but are not limited to:

1. Committing aggressive or malicious verbal communications or actions.
2. Inappropriate physical contact or sexual harassment.
3. Inappropriate comments to patients that reduce trust in the hospital or medical team.
4. Derogatory comments about the hospital's quality of care.
5. Throwing objects or instruments.
6. Impaired behavior resulting from alcohol or other substances.
7. Intimidating, threatening, vulgar, demeaning, disrespectful, discourteous language.
8. Disrupting Medical Center committees, department, or peer review functions
9. Inappropriate or altered medical records.

www.ingramcontent.com/pod-product-compliance
Lightning Source LLC
Chambersburg PA
CBHW070726220326
41598CB00024BA/3320